HOW TO GET
ABSOLUTELY ANYTHING
YOU WANT

IN SIX PRACTICAL, DOABLE, TIME-TESTED STEPS

BY

MARGIE ALIPRANDI

FOREWORD BY DENIS WAITLEY

TELEMACHUS PRESS

HOW TO GET ABSOLUTELY ANYTHING YOU WANT

Cover designed by Allison Hays

Cover art:
Copyright © Margie Aliprandi International

Published by Telemachus Press, LLC
http://www.telemachuspress.com

Visit the author website:
http://www.margiealiprandi.com

ISBN: 978-1-939337-41-2 (eBook)
ISBN: 978-1-939337-42-9 (Paperback)

Version 2013.04.02

Printed in the United States of America

10 9 8 7 6 5 4 3 2 1

For additional resources and PDFs of the exercises in
this book, please visit
http://www.absolutelyanythingyouwant.com

Praise

Get ready to dig deep, find your true purpose and leverage that into wealth. This book will help you to advance confidently towards your dreams and manifest your greatness.

> —Les Brown, best-selling author and motivational speaker

~~~~

I have known Margie Aliprandi for a long time. At one point she had very little. Now she has virtually everything, and she earned it all. She is proof that her teachings work.

> —Bob Proctor from *The Secret*, and author of *You Were Born Rich*

~~~~

Wealth coach Margie Aliprandi provides insightful tips and powerful exercises to help you create abundance in every area of your life.

> — T. Harv Eker, author of #1 *NY Times* bestseller *Secrets of the Millionaire Mind*

~~~~

This book is a must for everyone who wants everything from a bigger bankroll to a better love life.

—Dr. Joe Vitale, best-selling author and co-star of the hit movie, *The Secret*

~~~~

You can be anything you want to be. In How to Get Absolutely Anything You Want, Margie Aliprandi shares her proven formula for creating the life you want, and helps you bridge the gap from where you are to where you want to be.

—Sharon Lechter, founder and CEO of Pay Your Family First, annotator of *Outwitting the Devil*, co-author of *Three Feet from Gold* and *Rich Dad Poor Dad*

~~~~

A practical guide to getting rid of what you *don't* want and getting more of what you *do* want from love, work and play.

—Janet Bray Attwood, *New York Times* bestselling author, *The Passion Test*

~~~~

An inspiring and practical roadmap for creating the life you want.

—Greg S. Reid, author, *Think and Grow Rich Series* (*Three Feet From Gold*, and *Stickability*)

~~~~

Reading this book is like sitting down with your own personal coach who takes you by the hand and guides you through exactly what it takes to turn your dreams into reality.

—Marcia Wieder, CEO/Founder, Dream University

~~~~

I know Margie (business and personal) and would buy anything she wrote or recorded because somewhere in her content one would learn how she thinks, and that's worth millions. She doesn't pretend to help people; she helps them. If that's not the essence of business, I don't know business.

—Tim Sales, MLM multi-millionaire and producer of *Brilliant Compensation*

~~~~

This is a workbook on manifesting the life you love. Packed with great content!

—Randy Gage, author of the *New York Times* bestseller, *Risky Is the New Safe*

~~~~

It can be so easy to go through life on automatic cruise control instead of by design. It's never too late to take charge! From major overhauls to subtle yet powerful tweaks, you can design, plan and live your life as you choose. Because no one makes it alone, you now have this great book to help you. Quite simply, it shows you how to create the life you want.

—Sandra Yancey, founder and CEO,
eWomenNetwork, Inc.

~~~~

How to Get Absolutely Anything You Want delivers a profoundly important message for succeeding in business and in life. Margie brilliantly points out that success is achieved with and through specific goals, detailed plans and a relentless determination to becoming the best you can be. This is an important book that matters.

—Gary Ryan Blair, best selling author of
Everything Counts!

~~~~

Think life just happens to you? Think again! It really is possible to design and plan your life exactly as you want it to be. Margie Aliprandi guides you to do just that in *How to Get Absolutely Anything You Want*. She's helped more than 1,000 people become millionaires and create a life they love. Now it is YOUR turn. Get into this book today.

—Brandy Mychals, bestselling author of
How to Read a Client from Across the Room
and creator of the Character Code system

~~~~

Margie has achieved unprecedented success in the network marketing industry, with income in the one-percent bracket—an achievement that distributors and leaders admire. Bottom line, she has done it. Her authenticity cements their confidence in and adaptation of her time-proven methods.

—Richard Brooke, 35-year network marketing veteran and author of *Four Year Career*

~~~~

In these words you will find Margie's Magic. I happen to know that Margie Aliprandi manifested her own success by doing exactly what she outlines in this great work. This is a must read for anyone who wants to nourish their own genius within.

—Kody Bateman, author of *Promptings* and Founder and CEO of SendOutCards

~~~~

"Don't sweat the small stuff" when it comes to creating the life of your dreams. Buy *How to Get Absolutely Anything You Want* and start thinking big. This book is brimming with straightforward strategies to help you get whatever you want faster and more easily than you think.

—Kristine Carlson, success expert and author of the *Don't Sweat the Small Stuff* series with her late husband, Dr. Richard Carlson

~~~~

Do you have everything you want? Are you truly happy, fulfilled, healthy, wealthy and successful? If not, you must devour this book over and over again. It is a very precious gift because it contains the exact blueprints to design and create the most wonderful life imaginable and it will enable you to bypass years of struggle, pain, fear and failure. I wish I would have read it 30 years ago.

—Darshan G. Shanti, Founder of Freedom
Incorporated Inc. and author of *The 24 Hour
Champion – Discovering AND
Living Your Priceless Life*

~~~~

As a peak performance coach I know that success is predictable. There is a formula—an exact science—to getting whatever you want in love, life and money. This book simply and clearly outlines the process. Follow the steps, and manifest the life that you want.

—Brett Harward, speaker/author,
*The 5 Laws that Determine
All of Life's Outcomes*

~~~~

From this book you will gain absolute clarity about who you really are, what you really want, and how to create a fulfilling life of influence, affluence and contribution.

—Jill Lubin, international speaker and
three-time best selling author

~~~~

Aliprandi wraps you in a caring embrace while grabbing you by the shoulders and shaking you awake to what you must do to make the most of your life.

—Eva Gregory, author of
The Feel Good Guide to Prosperity

~~~~

If you would like to read a common sense, step by step approach to building a better life for yourself ... this book by Margie will certainly get you there a lot faster. Enjoy the read ... enjoy the ride.

—Mike Ferry, Founder of the Mike Ferry Organization, the Leading Real Estate Coaching and Training Company

~~~~

This book is dedicated to you,
and to the precious dreams that fill your heart,
and to the greatness in you longing to burst forth,
and to the recognition that whatever, *whatever* you
want already belongs to you
now.

Acknowledgements

Thank you from the bottom of my heart to everyone who has contributed to this book either directly or indirectly. From friends, team members, mastermind partners, mentors, colleagues and thought leaders to everyone in my family, your collective influence has inspired my soul, enriched my character, and illuminated brightly the pathways of my life's journey.

Thanks to my parents. Thank you Mom and Howard (my second father); and thank you Dad, who taught us to call you "The Lovely Daddy" from the moment we could speak. My dear mother Kay Ellison and my Lovely Daddy Robert Neil Christiansen, you raised us on the principles in this book. You led me and Charisse Orton, my sweet sister and sidekick, by example. You filled us with your love and you instilled in us the abiding faith that we could realize our dreams. Now here in your hands is the latest proof that you were right.

Thank you, Shaun, Nicole, Todd and Ashley for contributing to this book as only a mother's progeny could. Perhaps more than anyone, you have compelled me to understand and practice the principles on these pages, and I don't just mean patience and perseverance (smile). You came through the tests of becoming extraordinary adults with flying colors. Being your Mom has taught me life's most important lessons.

Because of you, I know unconditional love at the deepest level. You are my reason for living, and the center of my joy.

Thank you, Ray Zwisler, for your encouragement at every step; for being one of the few to read the manuscript cover-to-cover; for your incomparably valuable perspectives; and for being my precious partner and soul mate. Your belief in me never wavered, even if I doubted myself.

Thank you, my dear friend Bill Marshall, for likewise picking through every word and for your excellent suggestions—all simply from the kindness of your big heart.

Thank you, Allison Hays, my indispensable assistant, my treasured friend of decades, and the Empress of my life. Thank you for managing and holding everything together while I create. And for putting up with me.

And thank you, Elizabeth Miller, for your clarity and wisdom in guiding this project. As my dear friend and copywriter/editor, you have saved me from myself again and again, probably more times than I know. You have even made the process easy and joyful, except for those times that were so grueling and painful. And we haven't killed each other yet.

Finally, thank you to the great thought leaders in the field of personal development for all the priceless seeds and magnificent harvests you have brought forth to feed those who aspire to greatness in their lives. I have sprinkled your immortal words liberally throughout.

Thank you all. I love you all.

Contents

How to Use this Book | A Prerequisite | Start with a Clear Message | Break the INdecision Habit | Mixed Intentions | Make a Clear, Committed, Focused Decision | Clarify Your Life's Purpose | Your Definite Major Purpose | Your Core Values | Qualities and Character Traits to Bring More Fully into Your Life | Your Natural Gifts, Aptitudes and Favorite Activities | Your Life's Purpose | Clarify Your Goals | Get Your Goals on the Radar | To Be, To Do, To Have—That is the Question | What Do You Want?

What Are Beliefs, Anyway? | The Most Important Belief of All: "I Am Worthy" | How Belief Shapes Reality (and Lives) | The Good News about Beliefs | The Challenge of Choosing Your Beliefs | Changing Your Beliefs

Progress | Maintain a Constant Sense of Urgency | Whatever It Takes, Do It | The Razor's Edge Actions | Observe the Law of the Harvest | Persist | Masterminding as an Action-Taking Toolset

How to See Your World | The Vibrational Frequencies of Thought | The Ultimate Thank You

Foreword

When I first met Margie Aliprandi I knew she was special. Not only did I find her bright, creative, engaging and dedicated to helping others succeed; I soon discovered that she had learned and internalized the core concepts and actions that are authentic determinants of high performance human achievement. As I have followed her amazing career for many years, I have observed that she lives the principles she has written about. What impresses me most about her is that she is humble and approachable—always eager to share her knowledge with others as a great teacher who never stops learning and growing—no matter how much money and fame she has earned. She has never forgotten where she came from and who has influenced her on her climb to the top of her profession.

In this gem of a book, Margie offers you the "facts," not "fads" with clarity and in sequential steps that, if followed in earnest, will lead you to uncover your own gemstones, be they expressed by wealth or making a positive difference in your family, community or profession. She wants you to know and experience, in your own way, what she knows and has experienced during her incredible journey to peak performance.

I really identify with the six steps in the order she has presented them. Margie's Step One, *"Decide What You Want"* is a critical starting point. By doing an internal audit of your core passions and talents, you can take the next step to *"Build Belief"* in yourself and your mission. One of the reasons so few individuals really get what they want is that they never really decide, believe and focus on the intended outcome. She shows you how to *"Craft a Compelling Vision"* and then *"Think It, Speak It, and Affirm it into Existence."* Every Olympian, astronaut, entrepreneur, scientist, artist, and world leader I have encountered throughout my own career has done this.

There are two kinds of motivators: External and Internal. By far, the strongest, most dynamic motivators are those that *"Connect with the Heart."* Money, positions and possessions are external goals that drive us all. However, when your passions are connected to the heart, you can withstand the tests of setbacks and time and persist until you have reached your destination.

Margie's sixth step is the clincher. You can decide, believe, visualize, internalize and want success in your heart of hearts. But unless you *"Act"* and continue to act every day in some small way, you will be a dreamer instead of a doer. A decision is only a promise. It is true; everything we have invented was first a thought. Nevertheless, the world is full of permanent potential. Read this book, learn the steps, and go out and act upon these important teachings.

I am grateful for the opportunity to write a few words about Margie and this wonderful encapsulation of her life experience. I am grateful to be her close friend and colleague. And I know, as she so eloquently relates in Chapter Seven, that she is grateful for every blessing and accolade that has been bestowed upon her.

As a final note, I encourage you to read her introduction to this book. Too often, readers thumb through that section and go directly to the first chapter, eager to get to the action steps. By reading her introduction, you will gain a more intimate understanding, up front, close and personal, of the banquet of real life experience you are about to taste and enjoy.

—Denis Waitley
Author, Keynote Lecturer, and
Productivity Consultant

Introduction

Thank you for bringing this book into your life. I wrote it because I love helping people discover and unleash the powers they *already possess* to make the most of their lives. After all, in the context of all time, our presence here is like a tiny grain of sand on an endless shore. Doesn't that mean you need to pursue the best this life has to offer with the utmost urgency?

What is the state of your life today? What more do you want that would make it significantly better? What do you believe you want to contribute, achieve and acquire that could make your life fuller, more satisfying, or even a life of immense abundance in the time you have left?

I'm sure you already know this: You have the freedom, the intelligence and the capacity to dream anything you want to dream. You also have the ability to turn your dreams into reality. You are naturally endowed with the power to create. The life you're living right now is of your creation. If you could create your current circumstances, you can also create new and better ones. It really is that simple.

I want to dispel the myth that there's some secret to what is such a practical thing. I want to dispense with the idea that one needs specialized skills to achieve grand and glorious results. I cannot agree that there's some capricious god who has decided that he likes me today based on what I did or didn't do yesterday. I reject the idea that if I'm good enough I'll be rewarded with the things I want. I also feel that the widely-held concept of simply "ask-believe-receive" is incomplete as a formula for getting what you want.

Instead, it just makes plain sense to me that if you follow certain steps and do certain things and act in a certain way, you will in fact achieve commensurate results.

There *is* a formula for getting what you want. There *is* a process. There *are* specific action steps. There *are* some timeless principles that are taught, written about and practiced by successful people every day. Any thinking person can apply this to any rational, realistic goal. I can see it in the foundation of my own successes.

I had been a successful entrepreneur for years before I realized there really was a formula that could be learned and practiced to create the life I wanted. Until then I actually believed I may have just been lucky in the right place at the right time. And that was a scary place to be. If it was just "luck" or a certain "gift from the universe" at a certain time, how could I ever replicate a past success or teach others how to succeed?

As I attended seminars, read books and developed myself further, I realized I had already been applying certain common principles without realizing it. I learned that there's a specific anatomy to the creative process, and that it can be taught and replicated. Studying these principles and then sitting in seminars and hearing a story shared or a principle expanded upon I could honestly say, "That's exactly what I've already done! So now I can do it again!"

What a relief it was to find that it wasn't a hit-or-miss thing, that it wasn't because the stars were all aligned, and that it wasn't something that happened only to me and could never happen to me or anyone else ever again! No longer did I have to wonder, "Was it because I was being a good girl?" and "What did I do that made me so lucky?"

Oh, I should confess to having somewhat of a "special advantage," though. My upbringing left me open and eager to discipline myself in the quest of a fulfilling life. My mother was a model to follow, the way she managed her life and the way she never took "no" for an answer. She conditioned me with "You can be anything you want to be," and was always dedicated to creating opportunities for my personal growth and self-expression. Plus, my father was so into personal development that it was hugely responsible for the success of his real estate brokerage and his agents. I identified with the inspiration, information, guidance and recognition he lavished upon his team. He could motivate and inspire people to achieve more than they thought possible. This became what I wanted to do.

He gave me a reel-to-reel tape of the late Russell Conwell's *Acres of Diamonds* when I was nine years old. It was my first exposure to personal development material. It felt like "big people" ideas. I was honored that he gave me such an amazing gift and I listened to it over and over again. I became so aware and eventually so driven by the realization that our time is short, I started building a sense of urgency around "the moment," even at that young age.

I developed a tenderness toward people. I wanted to be able to lift them as I had seen my father do. I wanted to build a life of strong and definite purpose. I wanted to make a difference and help others do the same. I wanted to wring the most out of every moment and to be excellent in every area of my life, doing the best I could, being the best example, and taking the most heart-expansive right actions.

I wound up teaching from that foundation in one capacity or another from the time I became Miss Teenage Utah at age 14. That surprising event lead to speaking before youth groups and young women's groups on self-esteem, recognizing their unique value, setting high standards, expectations and goals, and how to be truly happy. Later I became Mrs. Utah and *that* surprising event lead to more motivational speaking and to serving as a role model to women throughout the state.

Singing with the Utah Opera Company, touring with the USO to entertain the troops, and acting in stage plays added extra layers of experience in my quest to make a difference. Stirring the emotions of an audience—evoking laughter, tears and joy—instilled in me a sense of contribution and the conviction that I could be instrumental in elevating a person's state of mind.

I so loved working with young people that I eventually embarked on a junior high school music teaching career. Yet it was short-lived because I was also raising a family and wanted much more time at home.

One day the opportunity came to combine the things I loved most: more time with my children, working my own way on my own schedule from home, being compensated according to my efforts, and doing what I felt I was born to do: helping people realize their fullest possible potential. I joined a fledgling network marketing company and built a team that is today about 250,000 strong in the United States and 29 other countries.

While personal development is among the requisites for any venture, perhaps no profession requires it more than network marketing. Even though this business model is based on people helping one another, its success depends on the willingness of independent individuals to banish their fears and disempowering beliefs, step out of their comfort zones, cross new frontiers of interpersonal relationships, remain strongly self-motivated, and lift themselves up by their own bootstraps.

So in order to grow that type of business successfully, you've got to grow yourself at a relatively deep level. I could see that pursuing a continuing education in personal development was a permanent necessity.

I asked myself, "What is the process of deliberately creating what we want? We know we're creating all the time—either consciously or by default—but what is that process? How do we take some faint idea that just sighs across the mind—that something we've been 'called' to do which is unique and personal to our being—and make it a reality in the physical world? What happens in the process to either advance or obstruct it?"

Looking back on my raw entrepreneurial beginnings I could see how I had traversed a specific evolutionary process.

First, a simple *decision:* Whether or not to build my own business, and to what extent. I was filled with doubts and fears because I was a single mom with three children; I had very little money; and I had no experience in business.

To even make the decision, I had to build some modicum of *belief* that I could do the work successfully. (And right here I must insert: my parents had never given me the negative money messages that would have sabotaged my belief that money is something I deserve.)

Once I had made the decision and built the belief that I could do the work, I moved into *action.* Next came more doubts and fears and sabotaging thoughts but I conquered them with more belief.

Building belief took *vision*—the ability to see the big picture of me becoming eminently successful and helping others do the same.

And so, I thought, that's how it's done. There it is. There's the formula. It's what I've been doing and it's what I keep seeing, albeit presented in various styles and levels of detail in seminars and in books.

You make a decision, hear positive and negative inner dialog, build belief, visualize, and act. You may want it with all your heart, but not know exactly what to do. But when you move into action anyway, that gives you confidence and feedback. You learn what works and what doesn't. This leads you to further clarify and expand your vision, and intensify your belief. And then, just as things start going well, you're sabotaged by your inner dialog. So you focus more on managing it, making sure it's in line with your vision and that you can see the silver lining in the clouds. Somewhere in here you learn to think, speak and affirm your goals; and you connect your goals to your heart.

As you start getting positive results, you start to love how that feels. Now you're no longer making hapless decisions. You keep performing more "right actions." And all of these steps overlap. There's obviously a constant interplay between them, all along the way.

I could finally pinpoint the six steps of the formula. I ran it by Bob Proctor, Denis Waitley, and a few other friends who are among the great thought leaders of our time in the field of success coaching and personal development. Was I missing anything? "No," said they, "certainly there are different ways to say things—but in those six steps you've got it all."

I started teaching "The Six Steps to Getting What You Want" in speaking engagements, conference calls and seminars. Soon came the requests for a book. And guess what. I found myself following the exact same decision-making, belief-building, vision-crafting, inner dialog-managing, heart-connecting, action-taking steps to write this book. Imagine that.

Yes, the formula for fulfilling your desires has been, is and forever will be expressed in different shapes, sizes and colors. My version is intentionally less detailed than others because I wanted you to have a simplified guide to a fast start, followed by relatively rapid progress straight ahead. Make it snappy! Make it urgent! Life is all too short! You can learn it, you can do it, and you can repeat it. You can achieve what you truly desire!

So I hope that by the end of our time together, you'll be inspired and motivated and committed to doing what it takes to live a fuller existence. The time-tested, tried-and-true formula is here. All it needs is you.

Margie Aliprandi
Salt Lake City, Utah and
San Diego, California USA
January, 2013

HOW TO GET ABSOLUTELY ANYTHING YOU WANT

IN SIX PRACTICAL, DOABLE, TIME-TESTED STEPS

CHAPTER ONE

Step One
Decide What You Want

Those who reach decisions promptly and definitely, know what they want and generally get it. The leaders in every walk of life decide quickly and firmly.

—Napoleon Hill

There you are, reading this book because of its title, because you hope it will help you, because you want to go beyond where you are today.

And here I am, entering your world through the printed page whose contents will help you find your way. No, speed you on your way. Until you stand tall upon that next plateau of your life, wherever it may be. You'll get there because you will have worked a six-step formula for getting what you want.

And yes you can learn it.

Yes you can master it.

And as you do, it will transform an idea from the first faint whisper of desire into resounding reality.

HOW TO USE THIS BOOK

Simply, you need to use it all. Each chapter contains one or more exercises. The exercises are self-examination and teaching instruments, and the chapters prepare you for them. You can't skip either one because:

- There's a gap—perhaps a wide one—between where you are and where you want to be, or you wouldn't be reading these words.
- You're not a "100 percent *deliberate* creator," or you wouldn't be reading these words. I think we can confidently assume that you haven't fully mastered the ability to create the roadmap of your life *by design*. I'll bet that in some areas, life is "just happening" to you. I call this "living by default." You're allowing something else (people, things, circumstances) to keep you from deliberately creating your life. Thus:
- You need to develop the habits that will put you in charge of shaping your own destiny. Habits that narrow the gap between where you are and where

you want to be, and that ultimately find you bursting through to whatever you want.

- The chapters will orient you and expand your understanding. The exercises will help you penetrate your inner self, guide your exploratory journey, and drive your learning to a deeper level.

For additional resources and PDFs of the exercises in this book, please visit:

http://www.absolutelyanythingyouwant.com

A PREREQUISITE

I said this in the Introduction and I'll probably say it again after this. *You can't attract what you don't have yet if you're not grateful for what you have now.* So before you begin, you must be genuinely and completely grateful for everything in your life as it is today.

But wait. This book is going to push you to think big, creative, expansive thoughts about wanting more. Whatever you aspire to. The sky's the limit. No holds barred. I want you to shoot for the moon.

So that might compel you to wonder, *Isn't that a contradiction? If I'm supposed to want outlandishly more, then how can I be grateful for the status quo?*

The answer: you can do both at the same time. Because you're hard-wired to do both. Both come from the same creative place inside you. The craving for more, the urge to expand, the longing for fulfillment—it's all simply the natural impulse to grow. So *the desire for more* is in your genes right along with your capacity for gratitude. They'll work hand-in-hand to your advantage as long as you give them equal billing in the theater of your mind.

It all comes down to this: Focus on lack, you get more lack. Focus on abundance, you get abundance. When you live your life in a constant state of gratefulness for everything *as it is,* you can then attract more.

So please begin with gratefulness at the very top of your mind. Think of every single thing you have to be grateful for, exactly as it is, today and every day.

START WITH A CLEAR MESSAGE

In this chapter you'll be challenged to answer the simple question, What do you want? What do you *really* want? Simple as it may seem, few people can answer specifically at first. I've met tons of them. I've been there myself. And no wonder. We all lead such busy, hectic lives as we run back and forth between life's different departments. We wear so many hats— the Family hat, the Relationship hat, the Community hat, the Employee hat, the Duty hat, the Performance hat, the Completion-of-Task hat and so on—that it's easy to lose touch with the inner self and the soul-based things we really want.

As you might guess, that inner self of yours is where you'll do the soul-searching. It's where you'll find one more thing that few people have seriously tried to define. But you, *you* are going to begin defining it here and now. Or if you've already done so, you may want to revisit and refine it.

That "one more thing" I mentioned is your life's purpose. Everybody has one, though it's often in hiding. But we do come with our own set of marching orders.

Once you've clarified your purpose, you'll be quickly on your way to identifying what you want, and making the clear, committed decision to get it.

Clarity—a crystal clear message of your intent—is everything. At every turn. At every step. Every moment of your day.

- Clarity of purpose.
- Clarity of goals and objectives.
- Clarity of decision.

Keep that in mind and strive for it as you go.

> *In any moment of decision, the best thing you can do is the right thing, the next best thing is the wrong thing, and the worst thing you can do is nothing.*
> —President Theodore Roosevelt

BREAK THE INDECISION HABIT

Of all the obstacles that so insidiously get in your way like humongous boulders rolling down a mountainside and coming to a stubborn standstill on the road in front of you, INdecision is usually the first one, right?

The word "indecision" seems to imply no decision at all. Yet we're making decisions all the time, either consciously or by default.

> *We can try to avoid making choices by doing nothing, but even that is a decision.*
> –Theodore Hesburgh

That must be why the Oxford Dictionary defines indecision NOT as the absence of one, but as "the inability to make a decision quickly."

Successful people make value-based decisions quickly and stick to them. Unsuccessful people take forever to decide, then change their minds many times. Look at all the time that takes. Time they can never recover. And more often than not, there are lost opportunities as well.

> *An unsettled mind is helpless. Indecision makes an unsettled mind.*
> –Napoleon Hill

Mixed Intentions: a Major Cause of Indecision

Between the decisive and the indecisive, which type describes you? If you're like most people, including me, one thing that makes it hard to zero in on making decisions is the presence of mixed intentions. On the one hand you have a strong desire to go beyond where you are right now. On the other hand you also have conflicting desires. You know, your "Don't Wants."

Like you Don't Want to get up off the couch because you want ease.

Or you Don't Want to tackle age-old problems that have been awaiting your solutions.

Or you Don't Want to pick up the phone for a conversation that might advance you toward your goal because you fear rejection.

Or you want a meaningful relationship but you Don't Want to put yourself out there.

Or you want to own a business but you Don't Want to take the risks.

And so on.

Imagine how many people buy gym memberships and never or hardly ever go. And how many want to be slim but just have to have ice cream. And how many attend weekend seminars, take a bunch of notes, buy expensive programs, and never even crack the wrappings. I think Tony Robbins says it's about 80 percent or more.

So you wonder what's going on here. The intention is there, but somehow it doesn't translate into results. I think a big part of it is this mixed intention thing where yes we want to improve and change and grow, but we also want the conflicting things that keep us from it. You know, like what's easy, what's safe, what's predictable, what's comfortable, and even what's more fun. Our desire for more doesn't always outweigh our desire for the comfort of the status quo.

So which intention will win? Whichever you want the most, that's likely the one you'll get. Just look at your results and you'll see whether you took the discipline to invest in your advancement, or you chose the status quo.

Regardless, humans are hard-wired to increase and expand. That instinct to excel and add value is deep within us all. And we have an opportunity every minute to make choices that will either advance us or set us back. Sometimes it goes unnoticed, but we're always either moving forward or sliding backward at every moment in every single area of life. It's just that simple.

You can't have both comfort and growth. Because growth by its very nature is going to cause you to step outside your comfort zone. It's going to make you stretch. It's going to bring up some fear. You're moving into the unknown. And that causes uncertainty while it also litters your forward path with those competing intentions.

Exercise 1-1
Confessions of My Mixed Intentions

Use this exercise to 'fess up to your mixed intentions. Your answers will show you which intentions prevail and what has prevented you from having what you wanted or still want.

In the left-hand column list three things you wanted badly in the past but never got. In the right-hand column list the reasons why you believe you never got them.

What I Wanted Badly   Why I Never Got It

_____   _____

_____   _____

_____   _____

Now look at your answers to "Why I Never Got It" and ask yourself, "Have I taken responsibility for this? Or have I blamed something outside of myself?" This helps you gain awareness of something that needs to be changed. All change begins with awareness. Take responsibility. Take control. Make things happen.

Please visit
http://www.absolutelyanythingyouwant.com
to download printable PDF copies of this exercise.

The Power of Indecision

Straddling the fence is painful, to say the least. So by the time this chapter ends I hope you will have liberated yourself from the gut-wrenching, debilitating anxieties and gyrations of The INdecision Habit and find yourself mastering the clarity of committed, focused, value-based, purpose-driven decisions that advance you toward your goals.

But first you need to recognize just how powerful an enemy indecision really is.

Indecision has the power to destroy.

One thing it destroys is clarity, which in turn leaves you sabotaging yourself right out of your ability to succeed.

I'm thinking of a woman I once met who complained that people weren't taking her seriously, and in some cases not even listening to her in business discussions.

I asked, "What do you really want when you're speaking with people?"

After a long introspective pause, she replied, "I don't know."

To help her along I suggested a few possibilities and then asked, "What's your goal?"

"I haven't thought about it," she confessed.

I believe she really had thought about it—surely it must have been "to make money" in her business—but she just hadn't seen the goal clearly enough to make a committed decision about it. And without that decision, she couldn't know which actions to take. Indecision had destroyed clarity.

By chance, would that be you? Have you ever found that you were putting forth the effort but the outcome you expected just kept eluding you? Have you ever felt you'd never reach some goal because your mind was jumping from thought to thought and you were in a state of directionless disorganization, just sort of wafting through your day? I have!

It happened one bright Utah morning when I was preparing to leave town. It was a classic example—albeit a tiny one—of the power of indecision to destroy clarity, create chaos, clutter the road with distractions, and prevent productivity.

My mind was full and running over with everything I needed to get done before leaving. One thought would send me to my desk, another to the bedroom, another to the kitchen downstairs. And on and on, flitting from place to place like a restless butterfly. At every destination, my mind would race ahead to the next one before I even finished what I had just set out to do!

Talk about distractions. In some cases I was so distracted by letting my mind run "fast forward" that I forgot what I was supposed to be doing at the moment. I was scattered, fragmented, and getting nowhere. I had been indecisive. My decision-making muscles had gone flabby. Until ...

Until I just slammed on the brakes and screeched to a stop. I thought, *For heaven's sakes, decide! First I'm going to do this. Then I'm going to do that. Decide and jump in. Just be present. Just be clear. Focus on one task at a time. No looking forward. No looking back.*

As simple as this was, it worked. It calmed me down. I felt the special peace that comes with being organized. I had clarity. And I began flowing smoothly from one destination to the next while completing my tasks efficiently. Once I clearly defined what I wanted and made a committed decision to get it done, I was no longer capable of being distracted. I had infused my activities with order, structure, productivity and achievement while the stress and anxiety vanished. As a result, I transformed desire into reality. What began as a thought became a tangible thing, which is where this book wants to take you.

Either you run the day or the day runs you.
                                          –Jim Rohn

MAKE A CLEAR, COMMITTED, FOCUSED DECISION

Oh, what power there is—what tremendous power there is—in a truly clear, committed and focused decision. The late Napoleon Hill called it "definiteness of purpose." In his seminal book, *Think and Grow Rich*, he wrote:

> *There is one quality which one must possess to win, and that is definiteness of purpose,*

> *the knowledge of what one wants, and a*
> *burning desire to possess it.*
> —Napoleon Hill

The word "decide" comes from the Latin word *de-caedere*—meaning, literally, to cut off. Yes it's also defined as making a final choice or judgment, or drawing a final conclusion. But most precisely, it means cutting the alternatives away. When you make a *true and unequivocal* decision, you eliminate every alternative from even the most fleeting consideration. You leave yourself no other option, no excuse, no back door, no out. You will settle for nothing else. Again, Hill nailed it.

> *Every person who wins in any undertaking*
> *must be willing to cut all sources of retreat.*
> *Only by doing so can one be sure of*
> *maintaining that state of mind known as a*
> *burning desire to win, which is essential to*
> *success.*
> —Napoleon Hill

Dr. Carole N. Hildebrand asserts that people have come to view decision as a wish rather than a commitment; and that we don't recognize what it means to make a *real* decision. She says "A true decision means you are committed to achieving a result." I couldn't agree more. Those who get ahead are those who make committed, non-negotiable decisions and then act on them—and it shows in their results.

> *Committed decisions show up in two places—your calendar and your checkbook. No matter what you say you value, or even think your priorities are, you have only to look at last year's calendar and checkbook to see the decisions you have made about what you truly value.*
> —Dr. Carole N. Hildebrand

Take a look at your calendar. Does it show that you routinely schedule time for personal enrichment? Do you reserve the first minutes of every day for the morning practice of reading inspirational material and meditating, praying, affirming or journaling? Do you make dates with yourself to set and review goals? Do you eke out time for physical activity and other life-balancing necessities? Do you attend personal or business development seminars?

Take a look at your checkbook. When was the last time you bought a self-development book or an audio program and actually opened it? Have you made firm decisions to take action on the things you've learned?

Take a look at your bank account. Do you see some positive results? Did you make committed decisions to invest in yourself and take action on your growth and your goals? I did and it does show in my bank account, year after year. I put my money where my heart lies. I'm investing in myself to be the best I can possibly be, and it pays.

Once you've decided what you want, you must not let it matter how many times you stumble or fall on your way to getting it. When you make a decision of high quality that is absolutely clear in your mind, it's as good as done. You don't have to re-think it. You will achieve this! You may fall 99 times but you'll rise 100, because you'll get back up and proceed with a whatever-it-takes attitude. You'll keep pressing toward your goal because your decision is non-negotiable. That's a clear and powerful place to be.

The act of firmly deciding applies equally to the small and big things requiring action throughout your life. Not all decisions are a big deal. Not all decisions require some kind of fanfare. But you have to make decisions regularly if you're going to live a volitional life. So you need to build your decision-making muscles. Even the little decisions count. They give traction to the bigger ones.

And even if you make a decision that turns out to have been the wrong one, don't be hard on yourself. At least you got feedback on what works and what doesn't. At least you've made the effort to move forward. That's better than being stuck in a state of indecision. You didn't let indecision wrench control away from you. You committed.

Until one is committed, there is hesitancy, the chance to draw back ... Concerning all acts of initiative (and creation), there is one elementary truth the ignorance of which kills countless ideas and splendid plans: that the moment one definitely commits oneself, then Providence moves too. All sorts of things occur to help one that would never otherwise have occurred. A whole stream of events issues from the decision, raising in one's favor all manner of unforeseen incidents and meetings and material assistance, which no man could have dreamed would have come his way.
– W. H. Murray

Did you get that? "Providence moves too." Wow! You receive help beyond your own efforts. Decisiveness and commitment equal providential assistance! Who can afford to miss out on that?

CLARIFY YOUR LIFE'S PURPOSE

Just as you were born with your own unique set of fingerprints, your own unique personality and your own unique talents, aptitudes and gifts, so were you born with a unique and specific purpose. You are an unrepeatable miracle.

Everyone has his own specific vocation or mission in life; everyone must carry out a concrete assignment that demands fulfillment. Therein he cannot be replaced, nor can his life be repeated, thus, everyone's task is unique as his specific opportunity.
                                  –Viktor Emil Frankl

What is that purpose? What are you here for? The more clearly you know the answer, and the closer your daily life aligns with your purpose, the more meaningful, joyful and contributing your life will be.

When you are "on purpose" there's a congruence and authenticity about you that's very attractive. You are in fuller expression of your true nature and calling. So you're happier and more joyful. This likely has a ripple effect across all areas of your life. And it benefits others in a couple of very productive ways. They're inspired by seeing you operate in full bloom. They may even want to emulate you. And they benefit from whatever it is you're contributing to this world: a new product, a new service, whatever it is you're creating.

And when you are congruent and clear—when you're really on purpose—the material resources necessary to the fulfillment of your purpose seem to make their way into your life. Chance meetings, new relationships, money—doors open.

Your Definite Major Purpose

What's the deeper reason behind your goals, objectives and activities? In my business we call this your "Why." It's something more than the money. It's something that's bigger, deeper and more meaningful to you. It's what Napoleon Hill introduced as "your Definite Major Purpose" decades ago as Lesson #2 in his book, *The Law of Success in Sixteen Lessons:*

> *The starting point of all human achievement is the development of a Definite Major Purpose.*
> —Napoleon Hill

Your Definite Major Purpose will motivate and drive you. It's what gets you out of bed in the morning. It's what keeps you going against the odds. It empowers you to find ways around those humongous boulders in the road.

> *When you discover your mission, you will feel its demand. It will fill you with enthusiasm and a burning desire to get to work on it.*
> —W. Clement Stone

Your Definite Major Purpose is inextricably bound to your uniqueness. And your uniqueness is made up of not only what you were born with, but also a set of four other factors that have shaped your life and who you are today.

1. Your core values.
2. Qualities and character traits that you want to bring more fully into your life.
3. Your natural gifts and aptitudes.
4. Your life experiences.

Those factors already reside within you. And within them are the keys to what your mission is. If you pull them out and get them on paper where you can see them clearly, you can best define:

- Your life's purpose.
- Your highest goals.
- How to live your life "on purpose."

So let's do that next, taking the above three factors one at a time.

Your Core Values

Your core values consist of whatever matters most to you deep down inside. They serve as your internal compass, guiding you consciously and unconsciously in the decisions you make about all of your activities and interests. They guide you in choosing your friends and significant other. They guide you in how you perform work, how you manage your household, what you do with your leisure time, and so on. Whether you're aware of it or not, they impact every area of your life and they influence your levels of happiness and fulfillment. Yet you may have never tried to thoroughly examine, understand, fine-tune and prioritize them. We call this "values work."

Getting clear about your values and what matters most to you is immensely important for getting the best possible picture of your life's purpose and your highest goals. With this clarity you will:

- Experience more power, purpose, prosperity and joy in everything you do.
- Find it easier to make wise decisions faster, and avoid making the wrong ones.
- Become clear about things that don't serve you and that no longer belong in your life.
- See where you are in the accomplishment of your biggest desires.
- Find life to be generally less complicated and more satisfying.
- Have more confidence.
- More easily draw the right people and resources into your life so you can design your life to honor the things that are most important to you.

Once you understand your core values at a deeper level, you'll be able to see whether or not you're living in alignment with them. For example, if you've identified "quality time with family" as your Number One core value and you're working 70 hours a week, you're probably not able to live in alignment with your most important core value. Ditto if you've identified "personal freedom" as your most important value, yet your job keeps you cooped up in a windowless cubicle and you're in a controlling, possessive relationship with someone who wants to dictate your every action.

Disconnects like these make it difficult if not impossible to be happy and live on purpose. And if you're not living in alignment with your life's purpose, you'll most likely feel incongruent, depressed, unmotivated, unproductive and unfulfilled. Values work can open your eyes to such disconnects and prompt you to make changes that can vastly improve your life.

The first time I formally explored my core values was in the early 1990s at a Tony Robbins seminar. I arrived feeling confident that I had a total grasp of my values because I knew what truly meant the most to me by age 15, and little if anything had changed by the time I was 30. However, the exercise he took us through was incredibly enlightening.

- Exactly which of my top values could I not live without?
- Exactly what did that value mean to me?
- Exactly what words would I use to describe it? Like, I had already identified my #1 value as "love," but love of what?

So the exercise caused me to precisely define the word "love" to mean "loving and being loved, love of family, love of a significant other, and universal love." This became my personal version of the word; a value that I would honor and live by.

Exercise 1-2
Elicit Your Core Values

Start your values work by using only your intuition and free-flow. Later on you'll see a master list of core values that may give you some ideas. No fair peeking now! Instead, please begin by free-flowing your ideas about your core values as you know them today. Ask yourself the following two questions over and over again until you've listed as many values as you can think of in no particular order.

- What do I value most in my life? (Example: Love.)
- What else do I value most? (Example: Financial freedom.)

Now ask yourself the following questions in order to drill down a little deeper. Your answers will help you create a first pass at your core values as you see them today.

- What gives my life meaning? (Example: Joy and happiness.)
- When have I been the happiest and most overwhelmed with joy?

- What value was I honoring then?
- When have I felt on top of the world?
- What aspect of my true nature was I honoring at that time?

Write your answers here:

_____   _____

_____   _____

_____   _____

_____   _____

_____   _____

_____   _____

_____   _____

_____   _____

_____   _____

_____   _____

Exercise 1-3
Fine-Tune Your Core Values

Now it's time for the "master list" of core values mentioned earlier. Look through the commonly used words below for words that may more precisely describe any of the values you wrote in Exercise 1–2. You might find words that express values you hadn't thought of yet. You might also see a single word that more precisely describes *several* values on your own list, so you might use it to consolidate them all. As you go through this master list, circle the words that resonate with you.

Accountability	Consistency	Empathy
Accuracy	Contentment	Enjoyment
Achievement	Continuous	Enthusiasm
Alertness	Improvement	Equality
Altruism	Contribution	Excellence
Ambition	Control	Excitement
Assertiveness	Cooperation	Expertise
Adventurous	Correctness	Exploration
Attitude	Courtesy	Expressive
Balance	Creative	Fairness
Being the Best	Expression	Faith
Belonging	Curiosity	Family
Boldness	Decisiveness	Fidelity
Calmness	Dependability	Fitness
Carefulness	Determination	Flexibility
Caring	Devout	Fluency
Challenge	Diligence	Focus
Cheerfulness	Discipline	Freedom
Cleanliness	Discretion	Frugality
Clear-	Diversity	Fun
mindedness	Dynamism	Generosity
Commitment	Economy	Goodness
Community	Effectiveness	Grace
Compassion	Efficiency	Growth
Competitiveness	Elegance	Happiness

Hard Work	Originality	Service
Harmony	Patience	Shrewdness
Health	Patriotism	Silence
Helping Society	Perfection	Simplicity
Holiness	Perseverance	Sincerity
Honesty	Personal	Soundness
Honor	Freedom	Speed
Humility	Personal Growth	Spontaneity
Independence	Piety	Stability
Industry	Poise	Strategic
Ingenuity	Positivity	Strength
Inner Harmony	Practicality	Structure
Inquisitive	Preparedness	Success
Insightful	Productivity	Support
Intelligent	Professionalism	Tactfulness
Intellectual	Prosperity	Teamwork
Status	Prudence	Temperance
Intuition	Quality	Thankfulness
Irreverence	Consciousness	Thoroughness
Joy	Reliability	Thoughtfulness
Justice	Resourcefulness	Timeliness
Leadership	Restraint	Tolerance
Legacy	Results-	Traditionalism
Love	Oriented	Tranquility
Loyalty	Rigor	Trustworthiness
Making a	Security	Truthfulness
Difference	Self-	Truth-Seeking
Mastery	Actualization	Understanding
Merit	Self-Control	Uniqueness
Moderation	Selflessness	Unity
Obedience	Self-Reliance	Usefulness
Openness	Sensitivity	Vision
Order	Serenity	Vitality

My Fine-Tuned List of Core Values

Now take the words you just circled plus the values you free-flowed in Exercise 1–2, and consolidate them here. This will give you a fine-tuned value list.

_____	_____
_____	_____
_____	_____
_____	_____
_____	_____
_____	_____
_____	_____
_____	_____

Please visit
http://www.absolutelyanythingyouwant.com to
download printable PDF copies of this exercise.

Exercise 1–4
Identify Your Top 10 Core Values and Prioritize Them

And now (trumpets and snare drums) the most challenging, illuminating and fun part of the process! In this two-part exercise, you're going to narrow your list down to your top ten values, and then rearrange them in the hierarchy of their importance to you.

A. First, look at your list of fine-tuned core values above, and ask yourself these questions:

- Which values could I conceivably live without? (Cross these off your list.)
- Which ones do I need most? (Put an asterisk by these.)
- Which would cause me the greatest discontent and sadness if they were missing? (Put a double asterisk by these.)
- Which ones matter so much that if I didn't have them, none of the others would matter? Examples might be "health" or "love." (Put a triple asterisk by these.)

B. Second, distill your top ten values from the above list and write them in the left-hand column below.

1. _____   _____

2. _____   _____

3. _____   _____

4. _____   _____

5. _____   _____

6. _____   _____

7. _____   _____

8. _____   _____

9. _____   _____

10. _____   _____

Now looking at the left-hand column above, you're going to prioritize those top ten core values by rearranging them in the order of their importance in the right-hand column. #1 will be the most important. You can either do this rearranging right on this page, or create a set of ten index cards, one for each core value. Lay out the cards on a desk top, and move them around until you've established their ultimate order of importance. Once you have the ten index cards in the right order, write their numbers on the cards, then write the words for those values into the right-hand column.

So now (whew!) you've clearly identified your core values. Congratulations!

Please visit
http://www.absolutelyanythingyouwant.com to download printable PDF copies of this exercise.

Margie's Results

Here's how my core values came out after putting them through the above process:

1. Love
2. Personal Freedom
3. Health and Vitality
4. Productivity
5. Creative Expression
6. Inner Harmony
7. Financial Prosperity
8. Personal Growth
9. Making a Difference
10. Adventure, Fun and Travel

Qualities and Character Traits to Bring More Fully into Your Life

As evolving beings, we have certain qualities and character traits that we have fully integrated into our unique personalities, and others that we're striving to add. So next we'll do a three-step exercise that will clearly show what they are.

Exercise 1-5
Who I Admire and Why

Think of your favorite people: anyone from your family, friends or mentors to great political figures, spiritual leaders, philosophers, authors, famous athletes—anyone living or dead that you admire, that inspires you, and that you want to emulate.

Then think of which qualities and character traits you admire most about each person. What is it about each one that you'd like to make a part of your character and everything you do? Some examples would be courage, authenticity, wisdom, knowledge, principled, visionary, honesty and trustworthiness, reliability, kindness, loving attitude, openness, light heartedness, poise, self-confidence etc.

A. In the left-hand column below, write the names of ten people you most admire and respect. Do this now.

Most Admired People	Their Qualities/ Character Traits
1. _____	_____
	_____
	_____
2. _____	_____
	_____
	_____
3. _____	_____
	_____
	_____
4. _____	_____
	_____
	_____
5. _____	_____
	_____
	_____

6. _____   _____
                              _____
                              _____
7. _____   _____
                              _____
                              _____
8. _____   _____
                              _____
                              _____
9. _____   _____
                              _____
                              _____
10. _____   _____
                              _____
                              _____

B. In the right-hand column above, write each person's outstanding qualities and character traits. Write as many as you like for each person. When finished you'll likely see that you admire the same things in several different people, and that's okay.

C. And now (more trumpets and snare drums) for the most exciting part. Claim these qualities and character traits as your own! Notice the duplicates. These are the qualities and character traits you want most for yourself. So the power comes in claiming them for yourself right now. My dear friend and abundance coach Teresa Romain gets the credit for this exercise.

- Simply write the words "I am" in front of each quality or characteristic listed in the right-hand column. (The "I am" is also a technique for creating powerful affirmations, a topic I'll discuss in Chapter Four.)
- Consider reading each "I am" statement out loud to yourself while looking in a mirror.

I can tell you that hearing these statements in your own voice is extremely powerful because of my experience with a similar application in a seminar setting. Sitting across from a partner, I would say "I am Margie and I am courageous." My partner would say "You are Margie and you are courageous." And what an emotional experience! So try the next best thing. Speak your "I am" statements to yourself in the mirror as a powerful way to claim your most-wanted qualities as your own.

Your Natural Gifts, Aptitudes and Favorite Activities

Okay. There's one more piece of the puzzle for defining your life's purpose.

- What are your special aptitudes, talents, gifts and passions?

- What do you love doing so much that time flies when you're doing it?
- What do you excel at?
- What do you do better than most anyone you know?

Exercise 1-6
What I Do Better
than Most Anyone,
and What I Love to Do in
Leisure Time

Write down everything you do well and everything you love to do. Here are just a few prompts to get you going.

Is it singing? Acting? Working with numbers? Working with people? Mechanics? Writing? Painting? Interior decorating? Organizing events? Brainstorming? Managing people? Computing? Selling things? Building things? Repairing things? What? Write down your preferences.

But don't just think of things you can monetize. Write down absolutely everything that you have a natural aptitude or affinity for. Is it cooking? Quilting? Water sports? Golf? Camping? Hiking? Biking? Traveling? Community service? Reading? If you weave it all together, it will all come into play as you define your life's purpose.

Please visit
http://www.absolutelyanythingyouwant.com to
download printable PDF copies of this exercise.

Now you're starting to clarify your life's purpose
evermore precisely.

I defined my life's purpose as the result of at-
tending the six-day Tony Robbins workshop called
"Date with Destiny" in 1996. As part of the course we
were to create a life mission statement. The final version was to contain an "I am" statement and an "I do"
statement. "I am _____, therefore I _____."
This identified one's life purpose. We were told to
make it as succinct and as powerful as possible.
Something that would resonate deeply and stir the
emotions if we said it out loud.

Even though I edited my original version several
times, it was still long and cumbersome. "I am a loving and giving being. I create inspiration; and I share
light, peace and harmony and create healing every-

where I go. Therefore I joyfully inspire others to live lives of fuller expression. This is my life's purpose."

Through the years I fine-tuned it, always keeping the ideas that originated in that workshop. When I finally distilled it to the fewest, most carefully selected and, to me, the most powerful words, I knew it had truly become my life's mission statement. I have never modified it since.

Now it cleanly and clearly states "The purpose of my life is to be joyful. I am love, I am light, I inspire others to live lives of fuller expression." That's it! Simple, yet so powerful to me. Yet those many years ago, I never would have been so bold as to flat-out say "I am love" or "I am light."

The point is it took years, it took clarity of mind, and it took a boldness of spirit that I didn't possess in the beginning.

I don't want it to take years for you. Hours or days, maybe. But not years. I want you to kick-start your journey toward getting what you want by doing your soul-searching and identifying and defining and clarifying and deciding right here, right now so you can get on with the rest of the steps pronto!

> *Don't ask what the world needs. Ask what makes you come alive, and go do it. Because what the world needs is people who have come alive.*
>
> –Howard Thurman

Your Life's Purpose

Why are you here? What sort of difference do you want to make? What song resides inside you that if you don't sing it, it will go unsung? Write it down here and now, concisely.

Exercise 1-7
My Life's Purpose
(My Personal Mission Statement)

Below, the "I am" is the set of qualities and character traits that I told you to claim as your own in Exercise 1-5. The "Therefore I" is what you will do—how you will utilize—these qualities and character traits to provide a benefit or make a difference. Again, the example I gave you earlier for my case was that I "inspire others to live lives of fuller expression."

Write your life's purpose—your personal mission statement—here:

I am _____

_____

_____

_____

Therefore I _____

_____

_____

_____

CLARIFY YOUR GOALS

So where are you in your life right now? What are your most important goals? What are the small ones? What are the big ones? What are your deepest, most cherished desires? Is it "more" of something like more self-confidence, more love, more peace of mind, more adventure, more money, more abundance all around? Is it a "better" something like a better home or better relationships or better appearance or better health? Is it more fulfilling work? Or is it less of something, like less stress, less weight, less fear, less self-sabotage?

Is it all of the above?

Or is it something far different from any of that?

Even something outrageously bigger? Like, what's your wildest, craziest, most audacious desire?

Just start thinking freely about all this as we go here. And think big. Go at it in your mind as if there were no barriers.

> *Dream no small dreams for they have no power to move the hearts of men.*
> –Johann Wolfgang von Goethe

And by the way. At this early stage, absolutely do not worry about "how" to achieve a goal. Just take comfort that you don't really need to know how. Because if you did, you wouldn't be growing. You'd be moving sideways, not forward. You must push beyond your comfort zone into places you've never been. You will be challenged. Celebrate the discomfort. This is exciting. Embrace it!

This is not yet about strategy or an action plan. When I ask you to write down what you want at the end of this chapter, it's only about free-flowing the possibilities so you aren't imposing any limits on the greatness you can achieve. So, don't say *Well, could I? Or How would I ever? And if I don't succeed, what would others think of me? Will I let myself down again?* None of that is the point here. You're just going to get your desires on the radar. If you knew success was assured and money and skill were not obstacles, what would you want?

And this is no time to be judgmental. Don't hamstring yourself by labeling any goal as silly, or impossible, or too big or too small. Every goal you come up with is important and unique to you. Right now the idea is to be carefree, creative and expansive. Please. Don't even try to be practical, logical, reasonable or realistic! To quote a line from the movie, *What a Girl Wants:* "Why do you try so hard to fit in when you were born to stand out?"

If there were no barriers, what would you really want? No matter how impossible the answer feels when it first crosses your mind, get it on the radar! If you do, you might be surprised that it becomes a reality. And if you don't, chances are that nothing will happen.

GET YOUR GOALS ON THE RADAR

When you've made that clear and committed decision about exactly what you want, there will be three steps to casting it in concrete. Or bronze, if you prefer.

1. Write it. A goal that goes unwritten is simply a wish.
2. Speak it. A goal that goes unspoken may never come to be.
3. Act on it. A goal you don't act on will leave you in the perpetual cycle of a life created by default rather than by design.

This simple formula—Write It, Speak It, Act on It—ordinary as it is, will put you in charge. It will make *you* the creator of your roadmap. It will turn your decisions into an unremitting force that has the power to transform a gossamer idea into tangible reality.

> *Write out a statement of your major purpose or definite chief aim. Commit it to memory and repeat it in audible words, day after day, until these vibrations of sound have reached your subconscious mind.*
> —Napoleon Hill

By writing a goal down, you are driving it into your psyche. You are giving it substance. You're taking ownership of it. You're deepening and strengthening its meaning, and your commitment to it. In the beginning, your goal was merely an ethereal idea inside you. Writing your goal down triggers its beginning as a physical form!

Then by speaking it, you're creating accountability. Speak it out loud. Tell someone. Tell several someones. Share your new decision with as many supportive, positive and encouraging people as you can. The more you hear yourself say it, the more real it becomes and the more muscle this gives you for getting what you want. Be specific about the details and put a deadline on it. Example: "I will move into my new home in Aspen, Colorado on July 1, 2020 at 9:00 a.m. Mountain Time." Now you're talking!

> *A goal is a dream with a deadline.*
> –Napoleon Hill

Set yourself some deadlines for *taking action* too. Some goals can be reached with just one action. Others involve a string of intermediate goals that you must act on systematically, one-foot-in-front-of-the-other and one-day-at-a-time along the way. Taking action is the subject of Chapter Six. As you'll see, you'll begin by deciding on the action or actions to take in the first 24 hours after writing your goal.

For now, understand that once you've made a decision—and once you've added to it the dimensions of Belief and Vision to be discussed in later chapters—you can literally Write, Speak, and Act your most cherished desires into existence. You can advance your decision from goal to goalpost. From idea to reality.

TO BE, TO DO, TO HAVE… THAT IS THE QUESTION

Being mindful that you need to create some degree of balance in your life, you'll be using the exercise at the end of this chapter to write what you want to Be, Do and Have in seven of life's departments.

Here are some examples in advance—small, large, and extra large—just to get you thinking.

Physical

- Be: fit enough to climb Everest, run marathons, become a champion swimmer, or just be at the top of my game every day.
- Do: walk 30 minutes a day, get a personal trainer, achieve my ideal weight.
- Have: abundant energy, excellent health, quality of life to the end.

Mental

- Be: humble, honest, disciplined, creative, principled, self-confident.
- Do: read the classics, read a book a month, learn a new language, invent a product, write many books.
- Have: a broad knowledge base, a sharp mind, recognition, fame, the Nobel Peace Prize.

Spiritual

- Be: strong, fearless, clear about my life's purpose, an inspirational leader.
- Do: meditate, read inspiring books, join a spiritual community.
- Have: a sense of "oneness," spiritual clarity, spiritual perspective.

Family, Friends, Relationships

- Be: more forgiving, grateful, loving, consistent, reliable.
- Do: make time for loved ones, be attentive to friendships, find the love of my life.
- Have: nurturing relationships, trusted friendships, better sex, children who obey.

Career and Money

- Be: highly creative, a big thinker, a business owner, a corporate CEO.

- Do: give it my all, advance my skills and knowledge, work toward a higher position.
- Have: immense wealth, or enough money to pay my bills; work that I love, no job at all (I want to fire my boss), stress-free retirement.

Adventure and Recreation

- Be: open, inquisitive and adventurous.
- Do: any kind of adventure, travel the world, jump out of an airplane, dive the ocean's depths, go to the moon, drink deeply of life.
- Have: broad and diverse experiences, balance between work and play.

Service and Contribution

- Be: influential, a servant, a teacher, able to give and share.
- Do: teach a skill, develop a class or a course, help the community, do volunteer work, donate to charity, share my experience.
- Have: feelings of accomplishment, the satisfaction of making a difference, an impact.

While these are only examples, my point here is that the order of things—Be, Do, Have—is the order you need to follow. There's a specific reason for this. Though simple, it's sometimes overlooked.

Deciding on the "Be" comes first because what and who you *become* in the process of reaching your goal is all-important. It's the anchor-point—the launching pad—for everything. It all ties back to your life's purpose. As you fill in the blanks of Exercise 1-8 below, and as you look back a few pages at how you described your life's purpose, I'm pretty sure you'll see a natural synergy and congruence between your purpose and who you want to Be in many of the seven life departments.

Makes sense, doesn't it? The idea is to keep you from approaching goals backwards as so many people do. Many people think only of things they want to Have. And that's just human nature. So they Do stuff and Do stuff and Do stuff in order to get it. Then they look at people who do have what they want. And they ask, "What are they doing? How did they get that?"

And so they start another cycle of Do, Do, Do. They might eventually get what they want, but they will have taken the long way around. They will have traveled a needless detour and wasted plenty of fuel. They began almost blindly because they hadn't been taught to discipline themselves based on a proven, systematic process, as this book is guiding you to do.

Here's the shortcut. The idea is *not* to ask "What are others *doing* to have what they have," but rather "What qualities do those people possess—what/who did they *become*—in order to get what they have?"

Then you want to focus on embodying those qualities, and moving into action. You will naturally Do the things that are necessary to ultimately Have what you desire. This is why the Be must come first.

WHAT DO YOU WANT?
GET IT ON THE RADAR

Big goals, little goals, great achievements—from little stuff you can accomplish in the short term to your most outrageous, audacious dreams, ambitions and desires—whatever you want to Be, Do and Have in any of life's departments, write it all down now. With abandon, tap the depths of your inner self, bring your deepest desires to the surface and fear not about writing them down.

"But Margie," you're probably saying, "you've been talking about discipline." And you'd be right, of course. But discipline begins with broad surveillance of the territory, then mining for all the nuggets and all the new beginnings that reside within you, just waiting to be given substance. And that takes courageous, nonjudgmental, anything-goes thinking to start with.

So for this first part of the process of getting what you want, you just need to get it on the radar. Write it *all* down so you can see it, and then sort through it, and then zero in on making the decisions that will launch you on your way.

Exercise 1-8
What I Want!

A. First, go back and review the sample prompts for the seven life departments under the title "To Be, To Do, To Have—That is the Question."

B. Then come back here and free-flow what you want to Be, Do and Have. Start with ten things you want to Do and Have in any area of your life. Then work backwards to who and what you must Be in order to make it happen. For example, if you want financial freedom, you may need to Be wise, disciplined, enterprising and consistent.

To Do and To Have: I Must Be:

1. _____   _____

   _____   _____

   _____   _____

2. _____   _____

   _____   _____

   _____   _____

3. _____   _____

   _____   _____

   _____   _____

4. _____   _____

   _____   _____

   _____   _____

STEP ONE: DECIDE WHAT YOU WANT

STEP ONE: DECIDE WHAT YOU WANT   47

5. _____   _____

_____   _____

_____   _____

6. _____   _____

_____   _____

_____   _____

7. _____   _____

_____   _____

_____   _____

8. _____   _____

_____   _____

_____   _____

9. _____   _____

_____   _____

_____   _____

10. _____   _____

_____   _____

_____   _____

C. Now go back to Exercise 1-7 and see how you described your life's purpose. I think you'll see congruence between your purpose and what you want to Be in many of life's departments.

Exercise 1-9
Choose One Goal from Above

Choose one goal that most resonates with you right now from the above list. Who do you need to Be to accomplish it, and what will you Have as a result?

WRITE IT

My chosen goal is: (example: start a new business)

_____

I will Be: (example: courageous, caring and consistent)

_____

Therefore I will Do: (example: provide exceptional customer service)

_____

And ultimately I will Have: (example: a business that yields substantial profits)

_____

I will achieve this goal by (when):

_____

SPEAK IT

I will share my goal with the following people in the next 24 hours.

_____
_____
_____
_____
_____

ACT ON IT

I will take the following action(s) in the next 24 hours:

_____

_____

_____

_____

_____

Decide that you will pursue this goal starting today. And once you've had the practical experience of taking this goal through the process from its infancy through to completion, you'll be able to repeat the process at any time for any goal you desire.

Please visit
http://www.absolutelyanythingyouwant.com to download printable PDF copies of this exercise.

The essence of life is that of personal growth; including emotional, spiritual, mental, physical and financial. All of this is a "natural" desire of humanity, and each plays its part in the creation of a full and complete life.

–Bob Burg

CHAPTER TWO

Step Two
Build Belief

If you believe you can you probably can. If you believe you won't, you most assuredly won't. Belief is the ignition switch that gets you off the launching pad.

—Denis Waitley

Congratulations! You're still with me because you want to Be, Do and Have more, and you're ready to make it happen. And congratulations on the in-depth personal work you completed in Chapter One. If you didn't complete all of the exercises, I encourage you to go back to them before proceeding. Working through them with care enables you to build the necessary and solid foundation for all there is to come.

The next step after that is to build a compelling and unshakable belief in your ability to make your dreams come true.

Beliefs have the power to create and the power to destroy. Human beings have the awesome ability to take any experience of their lives and create a meaning that disempowers them, or one that can literally save their lives.

                                    –Anthony Robbins

By the time you've finished this chapter you'll have a formula for changing and tailoring your beliefs to keep you moving in the right direction toward your goal. You will dig deep into your existing beliefs and identify which ones are irrelevant, which ones are empowering, and which ones need to be rethought and replaced with the empowering beliefs that can shape your new reality.

WHAT ARE BELIEFS, ANYWAY?

Simply put, beliefs are feelings of certainty. They are ideas that you've assimilated, adopted and given "legs" to. They are the only things standing between your conception of an idea and your ability to experience it, live it, and bring it into reality.

From the moment you took your very first breath, you began assimilating information to make sense of your world. You reached out to your caregivers, and you learned that by making certain sounds you'd get certain responses. From this you gained feelings of comfort and certainty.

As your brain developed into a thinking mind, you went about gathering ideas regarding the world, and life, and other people, and money, and love. Most likely you gathered from your family, from teachers, from friends, and maybe a religious community. The result essentially dictated what these well-meaning people believed was right and wrong. Some of it was useful; some of it "one-size-fits-all;" some of it not helpful in the slightest.

While you were still a young child, most likely you didn't have the capacity or desire to challenge those ideas. So as they just kept piling one on top of the other, it's only natural that you kept accepting and cramming them into a virtual backpack to be shouldered throughout life's journey.

For many, the most limiting of those ideas might have been something like, "No, you can't do such-and-so," and "You're not very good at _____" (you fill in the blank). And "Oh, you're just too slow, too late, too young, too old, too thin, not thin enough ..." whatever. If you heard any of those messages from people you trusted, most likely you believed them, either consciously or not. And into your backpack it all went.

The Most Important Belief of All: "I Am Worthy"

In the total process of getting what you want, there's one core belief that overrides everything. It's the belief that you either *are* or are *not* worthy of receiving all the good that life has to offer. One or the other of these beliefs resides at the roots of every action you take toward achieving your goals and will have a profound effect on your outcomes. So you must get this belief right at the very beginning of your journey. And stay alert to this always, because it could trip you up.

Sadly, many people are so thoroughly convinced they're unworthy and undeserving that they won't even let themselves *want* what they want! For them the result can only be paralysis from the start.

Then there's the opposite and equally disempowering extreme: those who take action in a frantic, frenetic sort of desperation to prove their worthiness to themselves. (This is much different from taking massive action that flows from a clear and strong sense of purpose.)

In between these extremes are people who generally accept their worthiness, but maybe not strongly enough to ignore the call of self-sabotage. If the belief that they aren't worthy and deserving doesn't jump in their way at the start, it often comes later, just when everything is going great. Especially when they're happier than ever in every department of life. That's when they can't help asking, "Gee, I don't know ... do I *really* deserve this? I mean, do I really have the right to be this happy in every area of my life?"

There's also a less intense version of those who have been tripped up by this problem. They simply settle for less than the maximum, way less than the big vision, and way, way less than the fulfillment of their Definite Major Purpose. They are resigned to accepting any outcome without striving for more.

Does any of this describe you?

If so, please know that until you really believe you really deserve what you really want, you're most likely not going to get it. No way can you draw the fullness of life to you if you believe you don't deserve it. This is a disempowering belief. And we have waaaaays to obliterate (smash, nuke, destroy) it!

There's a four-step process for uprooting and destroying disempowering beliefs immediately and permanently later in this chapter, but let's tackle this one head-on right now: You are worthy. Yes you *are* worthy. Yes you *do* deserve happiness and the things you want from life. They are your birthright!

Exercise 2-1
What I Believe About My Worthiness

A. Dig down deep for any sign of any belief that you don't deserve what you want. Then describe what you say to yourself, where you think that belief came from, and how you're going to turn it around to the positive.

I believe I don't deserve what I want because_____

_____

_____

_____

B. I think the origin of this belief is _____

_____

_____

_____

C. Take time for introspection here and internalize or repeat the following statement:

"I realize this is a false, self-sabotaging belief and that the happiness and fullness of life are mine by birthright. I am worthy of receiving what I want and I will declare this now and whenever I'm tempted to believe otherwise."

Please visit
http://www.absolutelyanythingyouwant.com to
download printable PDF copies of this exercise.

As you move through the steps in this book, you'll see all kinds of ways to retrain your subconscious mind so it gets this belief right. It's critical. It's the most important belief in your entire collection.

How Belief Shapes Reality (and Lives)

Because to believe is to feel certain, and because that gives you comfort, you build a foundation for a belief. You give it legs, and it walks along with you through life.

All the while you're looking into your past experiences for "supporting evidence" that your beliefs are true. And chances are you'll find it. When you do, it gives you comfort. I think this subtle habit of constantly looking for evidence is the catalyst of self-fulfilling prophecies, where beliefs shape one's reality. For better or for worse.

So that's how we become attached to our beliefs. They become more than passing ideas. We entrench them. We cherish them. Obviously they'll work for us or against us, depending on what they're made of.

> *You can be anything you want to be, if only you believe with sufficient conviction and act in accordance with your faith; for whatever the mind can conceive and believe, the mind can achieve.*
>
> –Napoleon Hill

If you can believe yourself into success, you can believe yourself into failure. Even if a belief is not in your best interests because it's the wrong fit for what you want to Be, Do and Have, the incessant quest for evidence that it's true can force it into reality. So of course you must be sure your thoughts don't trick you into choosing disempowering beliefs.

I'm reminded of an example that appeared like the proverbial 800-pound gorilla in the room. It was at a business seminar. I was sitting with a couple that had been building a business for nine years. The first thing they said was, "We haven't really had the business success that we want. People don't seem to take us seriously. We're still trying, but can't seem to get it together."

"Why is that the first thing you chose to share with me?" I asked.

"Well, we don't know," came the quizzical reply. But as I continued asking questions, the answer became clear as day. They had given legs to the idea that "People don't seem to take us seriously" and "We can't seem to get it together."

So I asked if they had any evidence in their nine years that people *do* listen to them and that they're actually very good at building their business.

"Well, yeah," they said—almost as if they were surprised that I'd ask such a ridiculous question.

I asked "Then why wouldn't you give legs to *that* belief?" And I said that if their experience included evidence of both failure and success, even if one is more dominant, why wouldn't they choose to give foundation to that evidence, and legs to the belief that would take them towards their goal? Why wouldn't they want to reinforce instead of ignore their past successes?

Without realizing it, they had glommed on to a limiting belief and it was blocking them from achieving their goals.

Just as their negative expectations seemed to be the cause of their negative results, my daughter Nicole seems to be getting positive results by expecting the best of the world around her. Sure enough, as in the exchange of a smile, the world mirrors it back. Perhaps the best example came about when she was studying abroad in France.

The French education system had gone on strike about halfway through the semester. She decided to turn this liability into an asset by taking a little trip through Europe "the student way," backpacking it and staying in hostels.

While waiting for a train one night in Spain, she dozed off and awakened to find that her backpack had vanished. Fortunately she had learned to always keep her passport in her pocket, but everything else was gone.

Finding a Western Union office or someplace where she could get a new American Express card was not all that easy. She was kind of going by the seat of her pants to find a city big enough where we could make those things happen. Of course this disrupted her plans, but worse, it could have embittered her against the world. Yet three days into the battle, I got an email from her that said "Mom, I just can't believe how wonderful people are. Everywhere I go people are helping me. I arrived at this hostel tonight. They gave me some free food and they're letting me stay here for free. And tomorrow I'm going to this town and I found out there's only one day of the whole year that this particular town has a festival and can you believe I'm arriving on that day. Life is just so good!"

As I read her words I thought, *You know, some-body could have adopted the belief that all Europeans are crooks, I've got to watch my back, this is miserable, this is disastrous.* But she was looking at the world through a different lens. She was telling herself, *People are going to help me, I can figure this out, I'll correct it as soon as possible, I hope that whoever got my stuff needed it more than I did.* And she was having a beautiful experience.

She concluded with "I just can't believe how beautiful life is and how great people are." And I re-member thinking, *And so it always will be for you, Nicole. Because that's what you're looking for. That's what you expect.*

What is it that you've been expecting? What might you be getting in return?

THE GOOD NEWS ABOUT BELIEFS

You get to choose them. You get to decide what to focus on. And what you focus on—whether it's in your best interest or not—becomes what you get more of. How powerful is that!

Do you have evidence somewhere in your life—even once—that you're exceptionally ambitious and you know how to get things done?

Do you have evidence somewhere in your life that you're lazy and that you procrastinate?

You have evidence of both, don't you.

So which one will you choose to give your precious moment-to-moment energy to? Will it be the belief that you're lazy and you procrastinate and you can't get anything done? Or will it be that you're ambitious and that once you set your mind to something, *it happens*?

If you've experienced even the most fleeting success at what you've wanted to achieve, and you think about it, give energy to it, and build belief around it, *this will take you toward your dreams just as surely as believing that you're failing can make you fail.*

> *Men often become what they believe themselves to be. If I believe I cannot do something, it makes me incapable of doing it. But when I believe I can, then I acquire the ability to do it even if I didn't have it in the beginning.*
>
> —Mahatma Gandhi

The Challenge of Choosing Your Beliefs

As mentioned earlier, I come from a network marketing background, where the business model is based upon building an ever-growing team of diverse individuals and teaching them to build teams of their own. It inherently involves an evolving process of self-development and personal growth for all participants whose common goal is entrepreneurial and financial success.

Early on I could see that to grow such a business I'd need to grow myself more comprehensively than had been required by any of my previous endeavors. So I pursued studies in self-development and leadership while observing the actions of successful people and tracking my own progress. I became at one with the ebbing and flowing tides of the growth process that you're seeing in this book: decide, believe, envision, affirm, connect to the heart, act.

I noticed that in practice, these steps were intertwined in a dynamically fluid way. While each step serves the other, rarely are they taken sequentially. Just as the painter dips her brush into one color on her palette, delivers hints of it to vastly disparate areas of her canvas, and then repeats that with the next and the next color as her design takes shape, so will you find yourself moving fluidly back and forth between the steps that cross through different parts of the process.

For example, you can make a decision and move into action while continuing to build belief. That action gives you confidence and feedback and you begin to craft your vision with more clarity and depth (Chapter Three). Sometimes it will be your vision that leads the way. Especially if your vision is stronger than your belief. Your vision may be so clear that it moves you into action straightaway. The natural, on-going interplay between these acts of creation helps you to get what you want.

That said, I've found that the process of *choosing* an empowering belief goes hand-in-hand with the decision-making step. From there, *sustaining* the em-powering belief is probably your greatest challenge. You have to keep it in sight. Otherwise it can succumb to disempowering beliefs that can remain entrenched for years without you realizing it, as was true for the couple at the seminar.

So you must stay constantly alert to the quality and character of your thinking. Choosing the best thing to believe in and then holding onto that belief is a skill that must be cultivated continually, as you'll see in more detail later.

Suffice it to say that self-sabotaging doubts, fears and limiting beliefs will pound relentlessly on the doorways to your mind. They'll loom up at every turn, often banging most loudly just when things are starting to go well.

I finally learned to face disempowering beliefs and replace them with empowering ones as a matter of routine. I would reach back for past evidence of a first-time success at *anything*, and use it to permeate my thoughts with proof that I could succeed anew at my current pursuit. Ironically, this same habit also impels people *away* from their goals if they choose to focus only on evidence of past failures. But by being very selective in the evidence I sought, I could arrive at the clear-eyed choice of a belief *and then retain it.* And that worked.

Perhaps the most stunning demonstration of this was when I saw it happen to a number of people in unison.

It was my tenth year with my parent company. I decided to try to earn a rank—Crown Diamond—that no one else had achieved. It would take a level of leadership, teamwork and team building beyond anything any of us had ever attempted. With my support, participating members of my team would have to grow their own businesses substantially in a fairly short period of time, as would I, so that each of us could rise to a higher rank.

Oh how I barraged myself with doubts of my ability to make it happen! For what seemed like an eternity I wrestled with both the decision-making and belief-building steps. No way could I *decide* if I didn't first *believe* I could actually meet the goal. I felt stuck because I was longing for assured success before I was even willing to move forward.

The goal was a very big one. When you have a big goal, there are times that you have to go back and build even *more* than the usual belief around it. I noticed that I was processing a whole new set of obstructive inner dialog. I had to language it with more specificity and connect it more strongly to my heart.

When I finally just declared aloud "I'll do it," I experienced a quiet sense of peace that set me confidently on my path. From there on, the power of decision animated everything. Team progress began almost immediately. All of us were holding onto the belief that we could do something that had never been done in the history of our then-12-year-old parent company.

We created a mastermind group (more about masterminds in Chapter Six). For four months we learned and grew together. We built belief in every single participant that they could achieve what they had declared they would achieve. Watching the beautiful interplay of these steps and the blossoming of results for a number of people at once was an experience that defies description. Even at the eleventh hour, some team members experienced results that no one could have possibly anticipated. Things happened "out of the blue" that we could only call miracles.

The result was not only that I became the company's first Crown Diamond. I had the joy of seeing 24 people do exactly what they set out to do as well. On awards night they all advanced to a rank that had only been reached by two people companywide the previous year! Thanks to the power of decision, and commitment, and choosing to cast aside their disempowering beliefs in favor of empowering ones, we had proven the process in spades.

So now I challenge you to never again waste your precious focus and moment-to-moment energy on beliefs that won't take you toward what you really want to Be, Do and Have.

CHANGING YOUR BELIEFS

What might you find in that backpack of beliefs you've been shouldering all these years? Is it possible that some are outmoded by now? Could it be that some have no basis in reality? Might some be outright disempowering? What needs to be rethought and replaced? What might be blocking you from your highest good?

Exercise 2-2 Action One Examine Your Beliefs

This exercise and how you respond to it will become a formula for you to quickly and permanently uproot and replace disempowering beliefs. It asks you to take these four action steps:

- Action One: Examine your beliefs.
- Action Two: Identify your disempowering beliefs.
- Action Three: Replace with empowering beliefs; stop giving your present moment energy to disempowering beliefs.
- Action Four: List your first-time successes from the past.

Fill in the blanks in as much detail as you can. Several responses are possible. Some may even be in conflict with one another. It doesn't matter. What we want right now is your first gut-level response. Be honest. Don't sugar-coat it or think you have to give "just the right answer." Spill out as many beliefs as you may have and just keep going. This way you'll soon see which beliefs are empowering and which ones need replacing.

A. What do you believe about life? For example, is life an amazing adventure that provides opportunity for growth? Or is life a hard test to simply be endured? Is everything going against you? Does it seem impossible to ever get beyond your current state? Whatever you believe about life, write it down with abandon, now.

What I Believe About Life

Life is _____

_____

_____

_____

_____

_____

When it comes to my life I _____

_____

_____

_____

_____

_____

In my life it always seems that _____

_____

_____

_____

_____

_____

My life is _____

_____

_____

_____

_____

B. Next, what do you believe about yourself? For example, do you believe you can really achieve what you want to Be, Do and Have? Or conversely, do you believe that no matter how hard you work, you're getting nowhere? Do you believe you're strong or weak? Do you believe you're good or not so good at what you do? And so on. Put exactly what you believe about yourself in your own words, here and now.

What I Believe About Myself

I am (write everything that comes to mind, and that could be a lot!) _____

_____
_____
_____
_____
_____

I always seem to _____
_____
_____
_____
_____

I wish I _____
_____
_____
_____

In terms of my ability, I _____
_____
_____
_____

When it comes to achieving my dreams I _____
_____
_____

_____

_____

_____

C. Next, what do you believe about people in general? For example, do you believe that most everyone around you is here to help and support you in the achievement of your goals and dreams? That people are intrinsically good and doing the best they can? Or do you believe that relationships are difficult, and that you've got to watch your back around people, being careful who you trust? Do you believe you're surrounded by love wherever you are? Or that people don't accept you? Or that you're getting no respect? Write it all down right here.

What I Believe About Others

People are _____

_____

_____

_____

Relationships are _____

_____

_____

_____

When it comes to other people, I find that _____

_____

_____

_____

_____

_____

People always _____

_____

_____

_____

_____

When I need support from people, they _____

_____

_____

_____

_____

D. Next, what do you believe about money? Do you believe that it's hard to make and easy to lose? That it doesn't grow on trees? That the love of money is the root of all evil? Do you believe it comes to you easily and rapidly from multiple sources? That money is simply an exchange for services rendered; a mechanism that measures contribution? That you deserve it or you don't? Whatever, write it down right here.

What I Believe About Money

Money is _____

_____

_____

_____

_____

_____

When it comes to money I _____

_____

_____

_____

_____

_____

With regard to making money I _____

_____

_____

_____

_____

_____

As a businessperson I _____

_____

_____

_____

_____

_____

Rich people are _____

_____

_____

_____

_____

_____

Now can you see that whatever you believe about these things becomes the prism through which you view the world? And thus do you see the power of belief for shaping the course of your life for better or worse? Remember, when you hold a certain belief, you instinctively look for evidence that it's true.

Exercise 2-2 Action Two Identify Your Disempowering Beliefs

Go back through and ask yourself, "Is that belief taking me closer to my goals?" Think through your negative beliefs. For example, did you say something negative about rich people? Do you by chance consider them snooty, dishonest and greedy, or just lucky? But you want to be wealthy too, don't you? Then realize that *you can never achieve something good if you have labeled it as evil or bad*. This disempowers you from getting what you want. So instead, *bless* whatever it is you desire. Acknowledge it. Edify it. Congratulate those who have it, and congratulate yourself for wanting it!

Now go back through Action One and circle every belief that could be obstructing you from your highest good.

Exercise 2-2 Action Three
Replace with Empowering Beliefs

Now it's time to choose or create new empowering beliefs in all these categories. To do so, ask yourself "What is the most empowering thing I could believe about_____?" Ask the question, pause, and the inspiration will come! Write down the answers below.

What is the most empowering thing I could believe about life? _____

_____

_____

_____

_____

What is the most empowering thing I could believe about myself and my ability to fulfill my desires? _____

_____

_____

_____

_____

What is the most empowering thing I could believe
about others? _____

_____

_____

_____

_____

_____

What is the most empowering thing I could believe
about money? _____

_____

_____

_____

_____

_____

What is the most empowering thing I could believe
about the goals I want to achieve? _____

_____

_____

_____

_____

_____

You've just created the replacements for your disempowering beliefs. When you direct your focus to
these more empowering ideas, they'll be the beliefs
you are giving legs to. And any belief that doesn't
resonate with any one of them is a belief you want to

dismiss. Decide here and now that you will never again give your present-moment energy to a belief that does not advance you toward your goals.

Exercise 2-2 Action Four
List Your First-Time Successes

The first-time successes in your past provide *evidence that you can succeed again* at getting what you want. Examples would include learning to drive a car, winning a game, getting an A on a spelling test, mastering a creative skill, earning an award, getting a promotion, receiving recognition, delivering on a difficult promise and so on. Remember the self-doubt, fear, pain, passion, determination and commitment all along the way—and then the joy of succeeding. And maybe even surprising yourself that you succeeded! Remember whatever you achieved. You did this! You can do it again! Note some specific instances when you were really proud of yourself. Make a list right here.

My First-Time Successes _____
_____
_____
_____
_____
_____
_____

The list you just created will be your *archive of supporting evidence that the empowering beliefs you're adopting are true*. You've just developed your own personal formula for changing your limiting beliefs immediately and permanently, and building the belief that can make whatever you want to happen, *happen!*

Please visit
http://www.absolutelyanythingyouwant.com to download printable PDF copies of this exercise.

CHAPTER THREE

Step Three
Craft a Compelling Vision

> *Dream lofty dreams, and as you dream, so you shall become. Your vision is the promise of what you shall one day be; your ideal is the prophecy of what you shall at last unveil.*
>
> –James Allen

Here's where I'll push you to be a bit outrageous. Along with defining your goal, deciding to pursue it, and building the belief that you'll achieve it, you have to be able to see it Big enough. You have to think boldly. You have to think expansively. There is no inspiration in small vision and small dreams. So this will involve the practice of *visualization* daily as a way to strengthen, crystallize and sustain your *vision* of actually getting what you want.

> *Imagination is everything. It is the preview of life's coming attractions.*
>
> –Albert Einstein

Imagination. What a gift. *A preview of life's coming attractions.* How profound. A visionary person has the imagination to see things that haven't happened with such clarity and intensity that he can bring them into existence and won't rest until it's done. Where else except from human imagination has any invention ever come to be, from the first crude tools of earliest man to the spaceships that have carried humans to our moon?

> *You have all the reason in the world to achieve your grandest dreams. Imagination plus innovation equals realization.*
> —Denis Waitley

VISION

Imagination *is* vision: this beautiful, unique ability that we have as human beings to paint pictures in our minds. Our eyes take in four million bits of information every second, and our imagination processes it all. We literally think in pictures. And we do it all the time.

Just as beliefs are intangible ideas that we give legs to, visions are intangible thoughts that we turn into images. The power of our innate vision is so strong that we can read the printed words in a book and transpose them into vivid mental pictures that far surpass anything Hollywood could create.

Have you ever loved a book and been disappointed by the movie? I remember reading *Les Miserables* and just weeping. I don't even know what I "saw" in those printed words, but when I saw the Broadway musical, and found that none of the characters fit the images I had envisioned, I thought *No, this isn't right.* I had a much grander vision. If you've ever had such an experience, you know exactly what I mean. The pictures you create in your mind can be so much more magnificent than anyone could put on the silver screen or the Broadway stage. So don't underestimate your visioning capacity.

> *Vision is the art of seeing what is invisible to others.*
> —Jonathan Swift

Vision lifts you over one of the toughest hurdles there is: breaking the bonds of constant focus on the current circumstances that you don't want, and mentally transporting yourself into "living" the circumstances you desire. You are naturally gifted with the ability to use this amazing power *at will* to craft a compelling vision of something that hasn't happened yet.

The compelling vision you create will become your own internal resource of inspiration and motivation. It will give you purpose. A reason for living. It will get you out of bed in the morning. It will inspire you to seize each day in bright-eyed anticipation. It will keep your spirits up. It will tell you how to plan. It will help you keep your eye on the goal so you don't get bogged down in the minutiae. Like a GPS in your car, or the North Star in the night sky, your vision will keep you on course to your dreams. And you're completely free to create, nurture and cultivate a vision of whatever you desire.

> *Create a vision and never let the environment, other people's beliefs, or the limits of what has been done in the past shape your decisions. Ignore conventional wisdom.*
> –Anthony Robbins

Your vision can drive you to greatness. It will propel you to make a difference in this world. It will push you past challenges and obstacles, keep you buoyant on the stormy seas of adversity, and help you succeed where others fail. It's the impetus that makes you reach beyond your comfort zone and do things that are new and challenging.

> *Be daring, be different, be impractical, be anything that will assert integrity of purpose and imaginative vision against the play-it-safers, the creatures of the commonplace, the slaves of the ordinary.*
> –Cecil Beaton

I can think of few things more important than crafting a clear and compelling vision of exactly what you want from the moment you mount your journey toward your goal. After all, how can you even set a goal without first having a glimpse of it, anyway? You can't. But your vision serves as inspiration to set goals that have a time frame and that are crystal clear, specific, measurable, realistic and attainable.

Those who can truly grasp the power of vision will forever change their relationship to life. We are not limited by our abilities or by our current circumstances. We are only limited by what we can see with our vision.

> *A vision is not just a picture of what we could be; it is an appeal to our better selves; a call to become something more.*
> –Rosabeth Moss Kanter

Sustaining Your Vision

Of course, it's easy enough to create pictures in your mind because, as we've acknowledged, it comes naturally to humans. But *sustaining* a vision and making it Big enough to work to your advantage is something else again.

How is it possible to sustain your vision if the state of your life today is far from what you want it to be?

How can you prevent today's conditions, results and finances from tricking your mind into believing they'll be just the same tomorrow?

How can you stop the "rearview mirror thinking" that prevents you from looking straight ahead? Of course, rearview mirror thinking is analogous to looking backwards instead of forward when driving your car. It means being focused on today's circumstances, all of which resulted from yesterday's thinking, habits and actions. Unknowingly and unintentionally, most people run their lives this way. Do you?

Ever since I decided to build my business, I have refused to look backwards or throw in the towel. But many around me did both when we encountered a series of three major crises over a three year period; all beyond our control.

When the first crisis struck I was well on the way to my first million. The entire company focus—thus every distributor's business—was on one hot-selling flagship product. But long-term use began to reveal that the product was unable to perform as expected. Boom. Thousands of customers and team members left in a matter of months. Those who stayed lost their momentum and became largely inactive.

In Year Two I was rebuilding my business when literally thousands of people, unable to find the success they longed for, decided to leave their company and join my team. I invested everything I had to get them up and running successfully and earning the income they desired. Yet after awhile it became clear that our company wasn't yet ready to accommodate the sudden growth that would follow. Over the course of six months, most of them trickled away.

In Year Three I had built my team up to 20,000 people when our company decided to change its name and asked everyone to sign a new distributor agreement. Boom! My team went from 20,000 to 10,000 overnight. Granted, 10,000 distributors is still substantial. I had retained that much of a team because I had persisted through rebuilding my business from scratch, twice.

I'm not telling you this as a "poor me" story. The point is that even though I didn't realize I was practicing the principles in this book at that time, I had made a committed decision, built belief around it, and was passionately sustaining my original vision no matter what. These principles, my commitment to my team, and my burning desire were seeing me through extraordinary events that were causing significant shock and awe.

I had viewed my decision to start my business as a destiny move. My goal was to build a better life for my children. All along I pursued it with such fervor, and my mind's eye was so fixed on my vision of it, that I saw these freakish events as mere blips on my radar. They never stopped me from eventually getting what I wanted. But by the time the third crisis hit, I was exhausted. So I took two years off to have my fourth child, and used that time to see if the dream of passive income would endure.

The tangible proof that my sustained vision had paid off showed up during those two years of "retirement" as a consistent five-figure monthly income.

And when I returned, I doubled my income in a year, and soon became the company's first Crown Diamond.

And so, I invite you to stop the rearview mirror thinking. Realize that we are all the sum total of yesterday's choices, whatever they were. With rearview mirror thinking, you allow yesterday's undesirable results to dictate how you feel, how you think, and even how you act today, tomorrow, and the tomorrows after that. But nothing says it has to be that way. You don't have to let past or present circumstances obscure your vision of what you can Be, Do and Have.

> *Create your future from your future, not your past.*
> —Werner Erhard

What's important is that you already have not only the freedom but the *capacity* to choose a new vision, apply new actions and literally craft a new reality in every area of your life. The idea is to master the ability to *sustain* that vision regardless of today's circumstances. That's where *visualization* comes in.

VISUALIZATION

Concisely stated, visualization is the process of creating positive mental images of something you want to happen in the future, and you carry it to the nth degree by seeing that vision as though it has already come to pass. You experience the feeling of living it *right now* in every detail, over and over again. You are bridging the gap between where you are and where you want to be. The bridge is made of the strong emotional connections that the visualization process builds between your mind and your heart; between you and your desires.

Once you see your end goal clearly, you can do what most successful people do:

> *Begin with the end in mind.*
> —Stephen R. Covey

I mentioned earlier that vision helps you plan. Beginning with the end in mind enables you to plan backwards from it, just as the professional golfer looks at the end (the hole he's aiming for) and plans his shot accordingly. He also flashes forward and "sees" himself actually achieving it. So begin with the end in mind. Make it a habit.

The Austrian neurologist/psychiatrist and Holocaust survivor Viktor Frankl, imprisoned by the Nazis in various concentration camps during World War II, used visualization to cope with the horrific conditions and suffering. Among his many visions:

> *I saw myself standing on a platform of a well lit, warm and pleasant lecture room. In front of me sat an attentive audience on comfortable upholstered seats. I was giving*

> *a lecture on the psychology of concentra-*
> *tion camps.*
> –Viktor Frankl

He wrote about the common traits a person must possess in order to survive rather than perish. He made a strong point that a positive vision of the future helps people endure discomfort, pain and suffering.

So I think it would beg the question, "What are you looking forward to? What's compelling that's on the horizon for you?" When people don't have a powerful vision of something that excites them—when they don't have plans for the future or a dream that sustains them through life—they can often enter a downward spiral and slowly die inside.

> *The only thing worse than being blind is*
> *having sight but no vision.*
> –Helen Keller

Thus it can be said that visualization can be used to strengthen and sustain a vision. But to many people it is infinitely more than that. To many it's the very thing that makes their dreams come true. The evidence is everywhere. And it can work for you!

> *We all possess more power and greater pos-*
> *sibilities than we realize, and visualizing is*
> *one of the greatest of those powers.*
> –Genevieve Behrend

So your next step in the deliberate creative process is to enhance your natural ability to:

- Create a crystal clear mental picture of whatever you want.
- See it as if it were already yours.
- See yourself enjoying it in every detail.
- See it with confidence that it will one day become reality.

> *I realize the dominating thoughts in my mind will eventually reproduce themselves in outward physical action and gradually transform themselves into physical reality ...*
> –Napoleon Hill

I've had several experiences that showed me the power of creating a personal vision and sustaining it to the point of reality. Among them was a fabulous trip around the world with my four children.

During several business trips to Malaysia I had fallen in love with everything about it: the culture, the food, the uniqueness of each region. And I had developed close relationships with people that became like family to me. I wanted my kids to experience all of it.

On one trip home I sat next to a flight attendant that had just been touring Thailand. She was so animated as she showed me her pictures from Bangkok and Chiang Mai. When I saw pictures of her riding an elephant, I just thought, *Some day my kids will do that.* I etched pictures upon my brain of me and my kids riding those elephants.

On some of those trips I had flown Business Class on the amazing Singapore Airlines. The gourmet meals, the outstanding service are just beyond description. Beyond compare. I wanted my kids to experience that too. And I etched that vision upon my brain. (As Bob Proctor says in his success seminars, you want to be sitting in the back of the car and the front of the airplane!)

Years later I learned of a flight package where you can go around the world for a certain price if you don't exceed 25,000 miles. I already knew exactly where I wanted us to go because I had been seeing the pictures over and over in my mind. So I laid it out dot-to-dot: Tokyo, Kuala Lumpur, Penang, Singapore, Sentosa, Thailand, Bangkok, Chiang Mai, then on around the world to the United Kingdom and then home. This added up 24,870 miles. It couldn't have gotten closer. And yes we would fly Singapore Airlines, in the front of the plane, First Class.

We had a wonderful time. In Malaysia my kids met the friends who had become like family. And ohhh, the foods! The foods they finally got to eat. Laksa, Nasi Lemak, and ice kuching, an icy dessert as delicious as it is beautiful. Most exciting of all was the bak kut teh, in the city of Klang, where it's better than anyplace else. Bak kut teh means "pork bone

tea." It's a wonderfully spiced meat and garlic break-
fast stew with a rich, thick gravy.

My children saw all the sights and they sampled
the richness of all the wonderful cultures throughout
our journey, but the most profound experience of all
was when we actually rode the elephants through the
mists of this beautiful lush green jungle in Chiang
Mai. It struck me like a lightning bolt that I had seen
this scene a hundred times in my mind before it ever
happened. I had never stopped envisioning any of
this. And now all the pieces of a grand experience had
come together naturally. It had begun as disconnected pictures in my mind—pictures that were like
seeds sown in disparate places but that germinated
and blossomed into the full reality of a beautifully
designed garden.

I can only compare that experience to the best
story I've ever heard about a popular aid to
visualization ...

The Vision Board

A vision board is simply a corkboard or plain poster
board that you fill with pictures, clippings etc.
relating to things you want. You mount it on a wall
where you're likely to see it most often.

Author-lecturer-business adviser John Asaraf created several vision boards over the years, and when
moving to a new home in California, he packed them

all into boxes. Those boxes remained unpacked for weeks after Asaraf moved in.

One day his five-year-old son asked him what was inside. Asaraf opened one and pulled out some pictures of things he had since acquired. He explained what a vision board is and how it works. He opened another box and what he found there brought tears to his eyes. Talk about being struck by lightning. It was a picture of the exact house he had just bought and moved into! Not a similar house. *The* house. He had clipped a photo of it out of *Dream Homes* magazine four years earlier! He said visualization had been working all along and now it had worked for his home. He was astonished to find that he had purchased his vision board dream home and didn't even know it.

I love vision boards because you can look at them any time, whether you're in a deliberate process of visualization or they catch your eye as you pass by. Thus their content can become indelibly engraved in your mind.

The first vision board I created was for a seminar assignment where we all bought several magazines, cut out pictures relating to what we wanted, and assembled them on our boards. I felt like a kid writing up a Christmas list. It was such a fun experience to find images that really crystallized the things I wanted.

I like a lot of travel and adventure so I included pictures of Egypt and the pyramids and guess what— we eventually went there. In fact to this day, I have never put any travel or adventure picture on a vision board that I didn't ultimately experience.

I added pictures of nature. And pictures of a woman meditating. And pictures of happy families laughing and having a good time together—hiking, boating, enjoying good food and wine and beautiful surroundings. I added pictures of love and romance. I added single words like inspiration, serenity, joy, unity, love, peace, laughter. And I did experience it all.

So I was encapsulating every area of my life and my desires on that vision board. It was an amazing experience and it gave me something tangible to look at.

Still, a vision board is filled with static images. You also need to create a movie in your mind that you can carry wherever you go, that you can replay whenever you want, and that makes those images sing and dance.

The One-Minute Movie

A colleague of mine, Richard Brooke, suggested the one-minute movie some time back. It's a very important visualization aid because adding movement to your mental images helps you sustain your vision. The idea is to design your movie so that you not only see your mental images in motion, but you also hear, feel, smell and taste anything that would engage your senses in reality. This way, your vision comes to life in your mind's eye in the greatest detail. It excites you and stirs your emotions. This helps you keep your vision forever fresh.

An Example of
One-Minute Movie Design

Keeping in mind that you'll make a movie about any-thing you want to Be, Do or Have, and since I am a total foodie, I'll illustrate the level of design detail I'm talking about with an example of two people joy-fully dining at a luxurious restaurant. Let's say you've posted a picture like that on your vision board. Now let's bring it to life.

Envision yourself dressed to kill and entering this fancy restaurant. The hostess welcomes you warmly. You thank her, say you're expecting someone, and ask if she has a table for two.

As she leads you to the table you absorb the total ambience: the background music, the soft and flat-tering lighting, the superb furnishings and accesso-ries, the perfect table settings, the voices of the patrons, the exquisite view outside and the wonderful aromas from the kitchen. You feel a twinge of hunger in anticipation of a fabulous feast as you stroll through the lovely surroundings.

The table is exactly what you'd hoped for: quiet, private, sweeping view of the city sparkling like dia-monds in the night, full yellow moon on the rise. You settle into the luxury of the deeply upholstered seat-ing. You take a deep breath and relax in all the com-fort that has embraced you.

Your eyes scan the elegant place settings, then move to the single red rose in the bud vase. You reach for the vase, pull it to you and inhale the bloom's perfume. You slide the vase back to exactly where you found it.

Soon your friend arrives and settles in. As you begin exchanging stories of how the day went, a crisply-aproned server arrives and pours tinkling ice water into your glasses. Soon you reach for the menu. As you open it your fingers appreciate the luxurious feel of its soft leather cover and the texture of the pages within. Your server reappears and you and your friend voice your orders. You each close your menus and hand them back to him. He tucks them under his arm and heads for the kitchen. And so on through your interactions with the server and your friend, the enjoyment of the delicious food, paying the check joyfully, and adding a generous tip. You get the idea.

And so, you must not just "think" your vision. You must literally feel it in every respect. Be as clear, concise and detailed as possible. And remember, your movie must have as its happy ending the scene of you having already accomplished your goal, and celebrating it.

Play your one-minute movie a hundred times a day if you like. And whenever you watch it, your subconscious mind won't know whether the unfolding events are actually happening now, or not. That's just the way it works.

Do you see the power that resides within you to potentially turn dreams into reality?

Nothing can prevent your picture from coming into concrete form except the same power which gave it birth: yourself.
                    –Genevieve Behrend

YOUR VISION IMPERATIVE

According to a well-known Bible verse, "Where there is no vision, the people perish." We can each apply this to ourselves. Vision is imperative. It has been so since the emergence of the human brain. It is the seed of every human achievement. It is the genesis of change and progress. It is the companion of hope. And it urges us to reach for more inside ourselves.

Vision is *your* imperative if you want to progress. And how beautiful it is that you already own this magnificent but underutilized gift! If I say, "There's a gorilla in your living room," what do you see? A gorilla in your living room? Of course! It's automatic and instantaneous. And when I say, "There's a bright pink gorilla in your living room," do you see a bright pink gorilla? Yes, of course. And when I say "The bright pink gorilla is wearing red slippers," what do you see? Of course. You've just painted the whole picture. So don't underestimate your ability to see Big things!

Now add the fact that you have a spotless future. No matter what the task, you have a completely blank canvas that you can paint on now! What to paint? The sky's the limit! *But the challenge is to be sure your vision is not influenced by your current circumstances—* unless, of course, you want them to stay the same!

How you see yourself is what you will become. You will live up to whatever vision you have of yourself. You have a vision of yourself as it relates to your work. You have a vision of yourself as someone who relates to people in a certain way, and that's going to impact your level of success in the outside world. You have a vision of yourself in your relationships with your significant other, with your children, with your bank account, with your health—and every single vision that you hold for yourself will determine a specific outcome. Why not expand it? Why not see it bigger and take the steps necessary to make that a reality?

If you can't keep seeing it you can't achieve it. So the first step toward the future you want is to develop your ability to envision it clearly, and the second step is to keep your vision alive through daily visualization. Let the following exercises get you started.

EXERCISES FOR CRAFTING A COMPELLING VISION

Introduction

The exercises you completed in the two previous chapters should have advanced you to where you've chosen one particular goal and started building belief in it. Now you need to tap into your beautiful, innate, *limitless* ability to create powerful mental pictures, and craft them into a compelling vision of your goal in the most exquisite clarity and detail.

The idea is to create *density* around whatever you desire. Remember, this whole book is about the creative process; about how you take a faint whisper of an idea through to its manifestation as a physical reality, adding density or substance each step of the way. Now you're going to give it specificity. This involves closing your eyes and envisioning exactly what you want and exactly how it's going to be when you get it.

As a warm-up, think about a time when you encountered some challenging, risk-taking opportunity that ignited unstoppable passion in you. For example: entering a new relationship, taking on a critical new work project, starting a new business, putting yourself to the test of some daredevil sport—whatever. My only point here is, that experience caused you to have Big, Expansive visions, didn't it. New hope. A flood of inspiration. And every one of those visions was of a future outcome that you hoped for. Think about that time. Remember how it felt. It was an avalanche of visions. It was an expansive feeling, wasn't it.

Did you feel like it was literally commanding you to raise the bar? Was it an appeal to you to reach your highest self so you could Be, Do and Have more? And in that moment, when you felt clear vision, Big vision, unstoppable vision—what kind of things were you saying to yourself? Can you remember? What was the internal dialog? Did it go like, "Oh my gosh, I can do this" and "This is going to be great"? I daresay, you were really saying positive things. That's the mental state you need to reach right now as you envision your current goal. Here goes ...

Exercise 3-1
Envision

I think it's good to start and finish your day in creative silence using visualization, maybe some meditation, and some affirming. You can use your vision board and/or any one of your one-minute movies as supporting visualization aids. And you can transport yourself from the cares of the day to the beautiful, glorious vision you've created for yourself in just minutes. Your subconscious mind won't know if your vision is real or imagined. But it's mechanically following your commands, and of course this is Nature's mysterious, unexplained process for the ultimate transformation of dreams into reality.

So let's get started now.

- First, create the ideal environment for visualization. Find a comfortable place away from any distractions. Get into a comfortable position. Close your eyes and scan your body for any tightness. Start at the top of your head. Be sure that your jaw is relaxed and your shoulders are down.

Then follow through with a scan of the rest of your body.

- Slow down, relax deeply, and don't force anything. Tune into your breath and just notice the gentle, natural rising of your chest and abdomen as you inhale and exhale. Pause slightly at the top and bottom of each breath to increase your focus. If a distracting thought enters, just gently release it and return to focusing your attention on your breath.

- When you're completely relaxed, begin to imagine. Choose to see whatever you want for this session. Anything from your most whimsical wishes to your deepest, most cherished, most unspoken desires.

What do you want to bring into your life? A new or remodeled home? A new car? A new or a strengthened relationship? A dream vacation? An adventure? An athletic triumph? A creative achievement? A trimmer figure? Better health? More self-confidence? The ability to deal effectively with a challenge at home or at work? The achievement of a business objective? More money? Total financial freedom? A life of infinite abundance?

Whatever it is, think boldly! Think expansively! But don't just think it. Feel it. See it. And see it Big.

Ask yourself these questions, and answer them all.

- How does this feel?
- How does it look?
- What sounds do I hear?
- What am I wearing?
- Where is it happening?
- What is the day (or night) like?
- Who's there and what are they saying to me?
- What am I saying to myself?
- Play the whole scene out in that brilliant, creative, imaginative mind of yours. Just go ahead and play it out.
- Now open your eyes and write down everything you envisioned. Give a detailed description that involves all of your senses right here.

What I Just Envisioned _____

_____
_____
_____
_____
_____
_____
_____
_____
_____

Exercise 3-2
Affirm

Write a positive, present-tense declaration of what you want to Be, Do and Have. Here's an example for achieving something that most people fear more than death:

"I am so happy and grateful that I am now an accomplished public speaker. I share my experience and wisdom with responsive audiences. I have confidence, clarity and poise."

Notice the Be, Do and Have in the above example. Now affirm your Be, Do and Have with crystal clarity here:

_____
_____
_____
_____
_____

Exercise 3-3
Make a Vision Board and a One-Minute Movie

(Note: You could also create a slideshow of your vision board in PowerPoint.)

For the Vision Board:
- Use a large poster board or a framed cork-board sold in office supply stores.

- Find five or six different magazines relating to different areas of your life that you want to make more abundant.
- Cut out the pictures that symbolize what you want to Be, Do and Have.
- Perhaps place a picture of yourself in the middle.
- Put the pictures on the board and mount it where you will see it regularly.
- Put a copy of the affirmation you just wrote on the board.
- Add some individual words that trigger satisfying pictures in your mind and stir your emotions (examples: Serenity, Joy, Fun, Laughter, Freedom, Leisure, Authentic, Celebrate).
- Add some relevant inspirational quotes if you like.
- Make it a habit to focus your attention on the board every day for 10 to 15 minutes at the very least.
- While looking at the board, immerse yourself deeply in your vision until you feel it in your heart.
- Idea for an overarching annual theme: In January, when you're thinking about the past year and the year that lies ahead, consider assigning a single activity to the pursuit of the goals on your vision board. For example, if last year was pretty much devoted to "foundation building," the New Year's theme could be called "action." Or if

last year's focus was "action," your theme for the coming year could be, for example, "bold and consistent action" or "expansion" or "balance" or "being present," "being mindful," and so on.

For Your One-Minute Movie:

- Create a movie for every area of your life in the grandest, most explicit detail you can conjure up. By answering the "Be, Do and Have" questions for the seven departments of life that I listed in Chapter One, you have already created a list of topics for your movies.
- By performing Exercises 3-1 and 3-2, you've already created the outline for a script.
- Now bring your script to life by applying the level of detail in the restaurant example to what you see in your script.
- Play your movie as many times a day as you possibly can. It's portable!

And remember ...

> *You only have control over three things in your life—the thoughts that you think, the images you visualize, and the actions you take (your behavior). How you use these three things determines everything you experience. If you don't like what you are producing and experiencing, you have to change your responses.*
> —Jack Canfield

CHAPTER FOUR

Step Four
Think It, Speak It,
Affirm It into Existence

*Every human is an artist. The dream of your
life is to make beautiful art.*

−Don Miguel Ruiz

All the steps in this book are about helping you
unleash your power to deliberately create your
most beautiful work of art: the person you want to
be, so you can live the life of your dreams.

The power is there in that magnificent mind of
yours, just waiting for you to use it *properly*. Of
course, you *are* using it every second, because it
consists of your thoughts, your words, and what
you do with them. But now the question is, *how*
are you using that power? Exactly what *are* you
thinking, which words *are* you choosing, and *do
they really support your most precious and
cherished desires*?

> *You must begin to think of yourself as be-*
> *coming the person you want to be.*
> –David Viscott

Thought is the birthplace of creativity. So there's never a moment that you're not creating. Your thoughts create your feelings. Your feelings create your behaviors, words and actions. And your behaviors, words and actions create results, for better or for worse. Most importantly, it's the persistently dominating thoughts and the incessant internal chatter—positive or negative—that will show up as your reality if you repeat them often enough. They have in large measure created your circumstances of today. They will create your circumstances of tomorrow. That's how powerful they are.

> *If we understood the power of our thoughts, we would guard them more closely. If we understood the awesome power of our words, we would prefer silence to almost anything negative. In our thoughts and words we create our own weaknesses and our own strengths. Our limitations and joys begin in our hearts. We can always replace negative with positive.*
> –Bettie Eadie

This chapter, then, is about the misuse and proper use of this innate and infinite power. I'll be laying out the problem statement and pushing you to develop the healthy thinking and languaging solutions that can help you create the circumstances you want. So far you've learned the foundations for this: defining what you want to Be, Do and Have; deciding to go for it; building belief that you can achieve it; and envisioning yourself owning it. Now comes the process of thinking it, speaking it, and affirming it into existence. Let's take these one at a time.

THOUGHTS:
WHAT ARE YOU THINKING?

Did you know that thinking human beings average 14,000 thoughts per day? That totals over 400 million thoughts in an 80-year lifetime—plenty of material to work with for shaping your destiny.

Unfortunately—perhaps because it's so easy—many of our 14,000 daily thoughts are re-hashed repetitions of what we thought yesterday, last week, last year, and worse, last decade(s). Some are thoughts we've picked up from other people. They aren't even ours. We just adopted them, and some may be myths.

Most of all, a great many of our thoughts involve incessant worry about the future and/or guilt about the past.

We so need to get control.

The Futility of Worry, The Futility of Guilt

Worry about the future—be it the next five hours or the next five years—occupies a very large share of our thoughts every day. Guilt about the past is another frequent visitor to the chambers of our minds.

How often have you built up a mountain of worry and climbed it over and over again without thinking *Wait! Stop! I'm just chasing a phantom!* Lots of times, I'll bet. And how many times was it all about something in the future that never came to be? Most of the time, I'll bet.

> *I am an old man and have known a great many troubles, but most of them never happened.*
> —Mark Twain

How many hours have you wasted feeling guilty about something you said or did in the past? You know very well that there's nothing that worry and guilt can do about the future or the past. You can play these thoughts over and over in your mind, but most of the future events that you fear will probably never happen; and feeling guilty about the past can't undo the past. For most people, self-imposed guilt trips only lead to a maddening maze of coulda-wouldashouldas and second-guessing the self. *How could I have reacted differently to So-and-So? I coulda done this. I shoulda done that. And what did So-and-So think of me?* On and on and on. My great grandmother, Martha Hodell, quoted this one often:

> *You wouldn't worry about what people think*
> *of you if you knew how seldom they do.*
> —Eleanor Roosevelt

Think of the hours you've wasted wandering around in that maze, drumming up imaginary conversations in your mind between you and So-and-So. You work yourself up to the point that you can feel it happening physically, even though you know it isn't real. When I stand back and see myself doing that, I crack myself up with how elaborate these conversations can become! They go on and on before I realize I've dreamed up enough dialog for a 90-minute movie. If it weren't so frustrating it would be laughable that we so unwittingly fall into this trap.

When you feel yourself slipping into the future or the past, stop! Slam on the brakes! Come back to the here and now! Now is real. Here is real. Give your full attention to the here and now. *The present is the only place where you can assert your most creative, most resourceful actions for getting the most out of life.*

> *Learn from the past, set vivid, detailed*
> *goals for the future, and live in the only*

> *moment of time over which you have any*
> *control: now.*
> —Denis Waitley

Worry, Guilt, and Energy Flow

While worry and guilt rob you of your precious time, they also steal the energy you need to change your life for the better. But if you focus on properly managing your thoughts, you're also managing your energy flow. And after 24 years in the health and wellness industry, I can tell you, most people have two priority requests: something for weight management and something for energy. They feel they're running an energy deficit, often because they're mismanaging the beautiful life force energy that comes to us all every day.

Think of your present energy as a bank account where money flows in and out. In this case, mostly out. It's a memorable mental picture that came from Carolyn Myss.

Let's say you have $100 in this bank account.

And you have an old grudge against someone. And let's say that by dwelling on this past grievance you're paying it $10. No big deal. He did you wrong! He deserves your wrath!

Then there's that disagreement you had with a co-worker last week. You get knots in your stomach every time you think of it. Another $10 gone.

Oh, and your daughter. She's skipping classes and hanging out with some questionable new friends. You can't shake the nagging feeling that you're in trouble. $15 gone to finance that one.

Then there's this awful guilty feeling about something you shouldn't have said yesterday. So by fretting over that, you're paying it $10.

Oh, and you're very fearful of the future. Maybe you'll lose your job. You might even lose a relationship. So by worrying about those two you're paying them $25 each.

Wow. Only $5 left in your bank account to finance the energy you need to accomplish something worthwhile today! By expending your energy futilely on future and past, you just don't have all the energy you need today—*in the present*—to create the life you want tomorrow.

Worry is not only a futile waste of energy; worry is the opposite of belief and trust. Worry is fear. And fear can't coexist with faith. So when worry dominates your thinking, you're stuck in a phenomenon that may attract the very things you're afraid of into your life.

> *All that a man achieves and that he fails to achieve is a direct result of his own thoughts ... As he thinks so he is; as he continues to think so he remains ... His condition is his own and not another man's ... His suffering and his happiness are evolved from within.*
>
> –James Allen

You are the Artist.
You Have the Power.

You absolutely have within you the power to change your life by how you think about it. There's nothing mystical about this. It's just a simple truth that we're connected with everything; the world is a mirror; and however we choose to think about anything, the world will mirror it back.

> *Thoughts are things! And powerful things at that, when mixed with definiteness of purpose, and burning desire, can be translated into riches.*
>
> –Napoleon Hill

Since "thinking it into existence" is a power that can bring you either what you do or don't want, steering your thoughts in the proper direction begins with the habit of constant vigilance. You must be so consistently tuned in to the nature and quality of *your most repetitive thoughts* that you become expert at choosing *only* those that support your goals.

> *By choosing your thoughts and by selecting which emotional currents you will release and which you will reinforce, you determine the quality of your light. You determine the effects that you have upon others and the nature of the experiences of your life.*
>
> –Gary Zukav

Thinking a goal into existence requires you to take charge of your thoughts and feelings and emotions. This isn't easy, but there are management strategies you can master, and I'll describe some of them soon. For now, the point is this: challenging as it may be, taking control is actually easier than staying stuck in an unfulfilling life, because your disempowering thoughts keep coming back to you as reality. Remember ...

> *Thoughts are boomerangs, returning with precision to their source. Choose wisely which ones you throw.*
> —Author unknown

This is huge. Nothing new, but huge. Every thought is energy. Literally, every thought is a force. Thoughts are not just pictures in your mind or emotions raging through your body. They vibrate outwardly from you. And every positive thought will attract a positive effect back in the direction from whence it came. Likewise, every negative thought will do the same.

> *I hold it true that thoughts are things.*
> *They're endowed with bodies and breath and wings;*
> *And that we send them forth to fill*
> *The world with good results or ill.*
> *That which we call our secret thought*
> *Speeds forth to Earth's remotest spot,*

Leaving its blessings or its woes
Like tracks behind it as it goes.
We build our future, thought by thought,
For good or ill, yet know it not.
Yet so the universe was wrought.
Thought is another name for fate;
Choose then thy destiny and wait,
For love brings love and hate brings hate.
                                        –Henry van Dyke

Wow.

"Thought is another name for fate."

That nails it in just six words.

Your thoughts are powerful living entities. So ask yourself: are they empowering or disempowering? Are they a service or a disservice to you and your dreams? Do they support what you want to change about your life? *Or are they keeping you stuck in unfavorable circumstances?*

When you start practicing conscious awareness and control of your most repetitive thoughts, you'll also become more aware of the words you're choosing to express them. Words will be the building blocks for affirmations; and affirmations make it possible to interrupt and reverse habitually unproductive thoughts.

Yes you can virtually rewire your thinking patterns and *think it, speak it and affirm it into existence.*

WORDS:
WHAT ARE YOU SAYING?

Your words are the wings of your thoughts, carrying them back and forth between your conscious and subconscious mind like boomerangs; and between you and the outside world like boomerangs. Your words are one of the most powerful forces at your disposal. So powerful indeed, that they can create or destroy.

Which words do you habitually choose to express your thoughts to yourself and to others?

Is your inner dialog helping or hurting you?

Does your external dialog help or hurt others?

And I ask again, *do your words support your goals?* Or do they attract the opposite of what you want?

> *The word is the most powerful tool you have as a human ... But like a sword with two edges, your word can create the most beautiful dream, or your word can destroy everything around you. One edge is the misuse of the word, which creates a living hell. The other edge is the impeccability of the word, which will only create beauty, love, and heaven on earth.*
>
> –Don Miguel Ruiz

The Words You Say
to Yourself

We all talk to ourselves all the time. We all have an Inner Voice. It's always dashing back and forth between three different behaviors:

- The Inner Coach or Inner Guide
- The Inner Cheerleader
- The Inner Critic.

Think of your Inner Voice as a scale that moves back and forth between negative and positive thinking. The Inner Critic would be on the far left; the Inner Coach would be around the middle; and the Inner Cheerleader on the far right. You'll be most effective when you keep the words you use and the "tone" of your Inner Voice in the middle to right of the scale.

When your Inner Voice is on good behavior because you've got it under control, it's a source of healthy constructive criticism that moderates your judgment and keeps you straight. That's your Inner Coach. Your reasoning mind. The wise part of you. It helps you evaluate a situation objectively with a minimal amount of emotion. This is your most neutral voice.

Your Inner Cheerleader is the one that encourages you, motivates you to take positive action, gives you self-confidence and endows you with a sense of personal power.

One of the jobs of your Inner Voice is to protect you. But in doing so, it often tries to insulate you from things that you really don't need to be protected from! This happens when you've lost control and the Voice becomes your Inner Critic. Now it "protects" you in the extreme. It can be a virtual demon that runs around in your brain like some out-of-control child bent on destroying everything within reach. If you don't manage it tightly it will saturate the words you say to yourself with all the negative, fear mongering, self-sabotaging inner dialog that can make you miserable, make you crazy, crush your dreams and block you from success. Obviously, then, the Inner Critic can be a very serious threat and capable of severe and lasting damage, depending on how strong it is inside you.

The Inner Critic usually speaks most loudly during a decision-making process, and again just when things seem on the brink of going well. It will always dance between helping you rationalize an issue, and overprotecting you from real or unreal danger, and overwhelming you with reasons why you flat-out can't succeed at whatever you're trying to do. The latter, of course, will cause you to fail if you let it prevail.

> *Failure is a trickster with a keen sense of irony*
> *and cunning. It takes great delight in tripping*
> *one when success is almost within reach.*
>
> –Napoleon Hill

So the trick is to "fire" your Inner Critic and "hire" both your Inner Coach and your Inner Cheerleader.

- When your Inner Critic says, "You'll probably fail," *immediately* say "Thank you for sharing. You're fired!" Then replace it with your Inner Cheerleader saying, "The only way I can fail is not to try."
- Whenever your Inner Critic says "You can't," immediately say "Thank you for sharing. You're fired!" and switch to your Inner Cheerleader saying, "I can accomplish anything I put my mind to."
- If your Inner Critic ever says "You're not (good, smart, strong) enough to do *that*," fire that thought and listen to your Inner Cheerleader saying, "I am (good, smart, strong) enough to do that! Within me I have everything I need to achieve my goals."
- And whenever your Inner Critic pushes you to beat yourself up over some mistake you've made, push back. Simply acknowledge that you need to improve, and make a firm commitment to do so.

Play this little "You're fired" game with yourself to keep your Inner Voice constantly positive in words and in tone. After you consciously use your will power to do this for a while, it will become a subconscious habit that you won't even have to think about.

Another way of dealing with your Inner Critic comes from psychotherapist Kali Munro. To soften the Inner Critic's power, recognize that you are not your Inner Critic. Yes it's part of you, but it isn't who you are. With this understanding, you should be able to step back and listen to your Inner Critic, but stand apart from it. By observing it in this detached way, you take the power out of its words and thus diminish its power over you.

And so, take charge of your Inner Voice and take charge of your life. You just can't afford to let a phantom compromise you and your potential for success. Your self-talk must be affirming and uplifting. It's imperative!

> *Your own words are the bricks and mortar of the dreams you want to realize. Your words are the greatest power you have. The words you choose and their use establish the life you experience.*
>
> –Sonia Choquette

The Words You Say to Others

Never lose sight of the fact that your words have the power to either tear people down or build them up and give them confidence and joy. Never forget that your words can change what others think of themselves, what they think of you, and how they treat you. That's how powerful your words are.

> *Be impeccable with your word. Speak with integrity. Say only what you mean. Avoid using the word to speak against yourself or to gossip about others. Use the power of your word in the direction of truth and love.*
> —Don Miguel Ruiz

When you were a child, you probably learned the phrase "Sticks and stones can break my bones but names will never hurt me." Yeah right. That wonderful saying has been handed down from generation to generation to help insulate children from the verbal bullying of their schoolyard peers. But after being called "ugly, stupid and dumb" and being told "I don't like you," many children suffer lingering and even life-altering consequences. Never underestimate the number of unhealed wounds in anyone's background.

You can choose to either criticize or be a voice of encouragement, reason and wisdom. Consider the words you speak to people that are closest to you. Are your words positive and encouraging? Or are they negative, critical and sarcastic, possibly because you're stressed and you're fresh out of patience? You could be in a state of utter frustration and say to a child, "You're lazy and you never do your chores!" Or you can summon up your utmost patience and say,

"Sweetheart, please go do your chores now." There's always a positive way to say it and get the best results for you both. Rather than labeling or categorizing, *just ask* for what you want.

> *Communicate with others as clearly as you can to avoid misunderstandings, sadness and drama. With just this one agreement, you can completely transform your life.*
> –Don Miguel Ruiz

Everyone needs to know that they're loved and respected and valued. Whether it's your family, friends, associates or pure strangers, make it a habit to remind them of their value with the words you choose to say. Realize how much you can positively impact people with genuine praise—not because you want something from them, but "just because."

Maybe it's a stranger that can use some kind words. Maybe it's someone you'll never see again. Or maybe it's the checker at the grocery store or the teller at the bank or the person that brings your mail rain or shine. It's just so worthwhile to let them hear an uplifting, empowering word.

Or maybe it's someone who pops into your mind when you're all alone and you start feeling love or gratitude for that person. Drop what you're doing, give that person a call and let your thoughts be known. Take action in the moment. It feels good. It builds strong bonds. It lifts the spirit. It warms the heart. It's a moment that might be indelibly engraved in the mind as a lasting memory. It can even be one of those moments that ultimately results in some life-changing event.

You never know what people are struggling with and how your words might buoy them through a day, a month, a year or a lifetime.

What you praise you increase.
                                              –Catherine Ponder

Words that Could be Better Chosen

The word "hate" is one of those words that deserves a better choice. We often hear "I hate it when that happens" and "I hate to say this but ..." and so on. Why keep such a harsh word in your everyday vocabulary? My children have substituted phrases like "I don't love it when that happens."

Here's another one. "Anxious." I used to say, "I'm anxious to hear what you think." But "anxious" can also mean uneasiness, fear or worry. That's not at all what I meant. So I swapped "anxious" for "eager." "I'm eager to hear what you think." "I'm eager to get together with you."

And except for every single "you have to" in this book (wink-wink nudge-nudge), let's get rid of "have to." Like, "I have to do this. I have to do that." This comes across as a sigh, a complaint, a "poor me." It seems like a victim's cry for attention and sympathy. We may not mean it that way, but that's often how it appears. Three positive alternatives are "I need to," "I want to," and "I choose to."

Oh, and then there's "I can't afford that." If you really want something, ask "How can I afford that?"

And "I can't do that." Instead say "How can I make that happen?"

Send your mind on a positive errand rather than dwelling on a negative idea. Use the creative faculty of your mind to figure out *how you can*.

Rummage around in that everyday vocabulary of yours and see which words you routinely use that could stand a switcheroo.

Exercise 4-1
Words I Want to Upgrade

Take a moment to think of words or phrases you'd like to upgrade, and write them in the left column. Anything at all that makes you cringe a little whenever you say or hear them! Then write your upgraded versions in the right-hand column.

_____   _____

_____   _____

_____   _____

_____   _____

_____   _____

_____   _____

Words that Erode Trust in You

In the movie *Bambi*, Thumper's father had it right when he told him, "If you can't say something nice, don't say nothing at all."

Okay, so maybe you're saying something negative about someone, and maybe he or she deserves it. And saying it may make you feel good. But this can boomerang on you. The person you say it to might wonder what you might say about *him* behind *his* back. He might even stop trusting you. Remember, what Peter tells me about Paul tells me more about Peter than Paul.

> *I affirm that nothing is as fast as the speed of trust. Nothing is as fulfilling as a relationship of trust. Nothing is as inspiring as an offering of trust. Nothing is as profitable as the economics of trust. Nothing has more influence than a reputation of trust.*
>
> –Stephen M. R. Covey

Words that Feed People's Problems

When people tell you their troubles, do you become an unwitting enabler by using words that only feed their problems and more deeply entrench their pain? Like "Oh that's awful! You poor thing! That's just *terrible!* I feel so sorry for you!" This is a totally natural response because you really do want to empathize, but doing it right takes a different choice of words.

What you really want are words like "I hear you! Oh my gosh that was difficult for you. I can't imagine how hard that must've been. And you're such a strong person, I *know* you've got the ability to overcome this. Let me know how I can support you!"

Be careful with your kind empathy. Stay out of the poor pity party. Don't use meaningless words that only dig an unconstructive path deeper.

Words of the Perpetual Victim

People who have a victim mentality will repeatedly voice their negative inner dialog over and over again to anyone who will listen. And then, even worse, they'll usually ignore any advice they get in return! Without realizing it, they're not seeking advice. They're seeking agreement that they're not responsible for whatever is wrong in their lives. They're "right!" They have been "wronged!" They are "powerless" to change it!

Not only does repeatedly voicing one's problems drive others away. It also drives those negative experiences ever deeper as the self-styled victim repeats them over and over again.

If this is you, don't beat yourself up over it. Like most people you're probably not even aware that you've fallen into this trap. It's an insidious habit that can sneak in under your radar. Your troubles *are* important to you, but don't let them become your story, your identity, your brand. You don't want that. There is a way out.

First, just don't tell people your troubles. It's totally useless! 80 percent of those people don't care, and, ha ha, 20 percent are actually glad to hear it! So make it a rule that you won't speak about negative or painful things unless you're dialoging with a coach or a dear friend, you need catharsis, and you're seriously searching for a solution.

Second, there are several specific strategies for reversing any negative thought/word pattern, and I'll be discussing them soon. For now, the point is *you can rewire your habitual thinking and speaking patterns.*

How Rewiring One Man's Thoughts Changed Several Lives

Damon is a dear friend of mine who changed his life and the lives of others by rewiring his thinking and speaking patterns.

Damon is a gentle soul. But for years he lived in a state of all-consuming anger, pain and resentment because he refused to forgive the man his ex-wife had chosen to marry. Damon's anger was so entrenched that it was affecting every area of his life including his children. They were confused and torn by being caught in the middle of a battle between their parents and seeing their father so upset. The last thing Damon wanted was to hurt his children, yet his thoughts and words were yielding the opposite of what he wanted.

When told by a friend that he really needed to forgive this guy, Damon said *Never.* But one day his intuition popped up and said *Wait. If I did try to forgive him, how would I go about it?* For some reason out of the blue he decided to ask for advice from a woman he worked with. She told him what to do in a few simple "rewiring" words that need to remain confidential.

At first Damon thought her advice was ridiculous. But finally he acted upon it. Within 24 hours he had translated her strategy into action. He sent a text message to this guy that he resented so much. Essentially it said *We have to stop this. It's hurting the kids, and I want to sit down with you and Kathy.*

This one inspired action changed everything in a week. It marked a massive change in Damon's everyday thoughts, words and emotions. It totally softened the children, the ex-wife, and the man that Damon thought he could never forgive. Now Damon doesn't meet with resistance when he wants to spend extra time with his kids. They're at peace with the situation and they get to see their Dad taking the high road. The healing that came from changing one person's thoughts and words had a permanent ripple effect on everyone involved.

> *When you hold resentment toward another*
> *you are bound to that person or condition*

by an emotional link that is stronger than steel. Forgiveness is the only way to dissolve that link and get free.
                                   –Catherine Ponder

It all comes back to the idea of consciously creating your reality. We all have the power to change a thought pattern—no matter how deeply entrenched—and to flip it 180 degrees until it becomes the beneficial reality we seek.

Forgiveness—the forgiving state of mind—is a magnetic power for attracting good.
                                   –Catherine Ponder

Yes you do have the power to change your beliefs, your life, and even the lives of others, by changing your thoughts and your words.

SIMPLE STRATEGIES FOR CHANGE

If we're really going to get what we want, we must not only know ourselves. We must also honor ourselves, identify every little thought that repeats itself, and understand every emotion that drives us.

Every emotion is a message from the soul. Every emotion is a reaction to a thought. So we must stay constantly aware of what's on our emotional landscape.

While most of us are good at diverting our attention from our emotions, we need to do the opposite. We need to pay attention to our emotions because they give us such useful information about ourselves.

When I first decided I wanted to discipline myself to be truly aware of what I was thinking at all times, it seemed hugely ambitious—if not impossible—because I have such an active mind. Yet to my surprise it wasn't long before I did become really tuned in. I learned several strategies for facing my emotions, identifying their sources, and deliberately choosing my thoughts rather than letting them run randomly through me. Here are some of those strategies.

Use Your Body as a Teacher

When a negative thought goes rogue and you have an intense emotional reaction to it, it's going to show up somewhere in your body. Indeed, this is a prime example of thoughts becoming things.

Next time you have such an experience, just pause, honor yourself, observe what you're feeling, and allow yourself to feel it. Does your throat tighten up? Is there a pit in your stomach? Got sweaty palms? A face that's on fire? A weight on your chest? Tune in to these visceral responses. Your body is alerting you to the presence of emotions that need your attention.

By tuning in to your physical reactions, you can usually trace them back to the thought impulse where it all began. Then you can become aware of your emotional patterns and identify the very thoughts and words that set your emotions reeling. Once you've connected those dots, you can choose more empowering thoughts that relieve stress, support your health, elevate your mood and create comfortable physical feelings.

What will you find on this voyage of vigilance? What's on your emotional landscape? How are you re-acting to the thoughts that have turned into un-healthy physical feelings? Is there a pattern to it all? See what you need to change so you can gain more control of your thinking patterns and emotions.

Accept and Surrender

This is where you accept that there are some things you simply can't control and/or change at the present moment. So there's nothing left except surrender. Not as a defeatist, but with the wisdom to acknowledge that the rest of the story is yet to be told. The sooner you do this, the better. Continued resistance only wastes time and energy and prevents you from turning to productive paths. Damon's story was an example.

- Surrender to the idea that there may be something divine at work that's entirely apart from everything you can see and understand.

- Trust that there may be a larger purpose that you simply aren't comprehending.
- Accept the dashing of your hopes and the unfulfilled expectations, devastating as they are.
- Go with the twists and turns on the Street of Expectations as unavoidable detours that may ultimately be for your best good, even though you can't yet see where they lead.
- Surrender to the love that's surrounding you right now.

I'm reminded of the I-Ching and the zigzag path. The I-Ching says that nature takes a zigzag path to its goals. And there are always miracles along the path that we can't see until their time. You know what you want, but you don't have a detailed roadmap with all the twists and turns en route.

The human ego always wants certainty. It wants to understand everything right now. It likes to see a straight line from where we are to where we want to be. But that's not the path of the divine. The path of the divine is a zigzag path. So it meanders out of view. And that scares us. Yet we can allay those fears. We can even stop rogue thoughts in their tracks if we'll simply trust, accept and surrender to events that we can't control.

Use Mother Nature as a Teacher

I especially love this one. Look for lessons from Nature. There's a tree outside my bedroom picture window that I routinely use as my teacher. I'll look out at it and think, *Isn't it interesting, how the leaves just simply do their thing.* Sometimes they stand still. Sometimes they move in shimmering excitement. Sometimes they're green; sometimes they're yellow as they come and go with the seasons. They don't have a bad day. They don't resist. They just always go with the flow.

I ask, *Can I not be more like the leaves? We're made of the same stuff, so what's all my resistance about?* And I draw tremendous strength from these sweet gifts of Mother Nature. If I calm myself as I watch them, I can feel my breathing become more relaxed and my tensions disappear.

One day when it seemed that nothing was going my way, I finally realized I had been resisting instead of surrendering to things I couldn't control. Suddenly I thought, *My leaves! I'm going to go upstairs and watch my leaves!*

I ran up the stairs and looked out and they were gone! They'd been there the day before, ready to give in to the cold. Strong winds overnight had suddenly blown them away.

The lesson that came back to me? A different season had taken over and the leaves surrendered to it. Why? Because it was a cycle of life and for the good of the tree. Nature made some trees that can only survive by sleeping through the cold and storing energy in their roots so they can renew their leaves come spring.

And that was my answer too.

My resistance had been for naught. It was not yet the season for what I wanted.

So it was time to surrender ... to redirect myself to more productive pursuits ... to push my roots a little deeper and to strengthen them for what was to come. Just as that tree does when it must.

Be Grateful

As I mentioned up front, you can't attract what you don't have yet if you're not grateful for what you have right now. Since the attitude of gratitude is the overarching concept for getting what you want, it's especially useful when you need to counteract worry and stabilize troublesome emotions. No matter how dismal things may seem, you can always find something to be very, very grateful for. More about gratefulness in Chapter Seven.

Unplug

I especially love this one from Carolyn Myss, and I use it all the time.

When you identify a habitual thought pattern that just screams to be stopped because it's distracting you and it's upsetting you emotionally, saying "I unplug" works wonders.

The idea is to picture your unsupportive, worry-laden thought patterns as electrical current flowing through a cable that's plugged into a wall socket. Say "I unplug!" as you "see" yourself rrripping that plug right out of the wall and instantly ending the life of whatever it was connected to.

I think "I unplug!" is way better than "Stop!" because "Stop!" doesn't prevent you from starting again! But "I unplug!" is final. By pulling the plug, you're cutting off all the energy to your unwanted emotions.

Say *I unplug! I refuse to perpetuate and animate that thought with my emotions!*

Until Now

This one works for interrupting the habitual thinking that throws you into a downward spiral of self-criticism and the debilitating emotional reactions that come with it.

Here you're applying and directing the power of your magnificent mind to turn negatives into positives by saying "until now" whenever you catch your Inner Critic in the act of putting you down.

Maybe my Inner Critic says "Margie, you're not very good at _____!" or "Margie, you've *never* been able to _____!"

If I just let those criticisms go in one ear and out the other instead of interrupting them, they're going to keep coming baaaaack; they'll convince me that I'm really no good at whatever; and they'll eventually disempower me.

I'm not going to let that happen. By adding the words "until now!" to *any* negative inner dialog, I've changed the energy of my whole being. I've taken a clean, clear, *non-judgmental* stance that snaps me awake to the positive. I'm owning up to the existence of something I need to fix; I make a commitment to fix it; and I put a *solution* into motion. "Margie, you've never been able to _____, until now."

AFFIRMATIONS: THE CROWN JEWEL OF SOLUTIONS

My friend and mentor Bob Proctor says there are two ways to create lasting change. One is a catastrophic life event, and the other is the consistent repetition of new information. The latter, of course, refers to affirmations. While inviting you to dip a toe into these waters earlier, I've been saving the in-depth discussion until now.

The word "affirmation" comes from "affirm," which means to make firm. When you repeat anything to yourself over and over again, negative or positive, you are affirming that thought.

Intrinsically speaking, your dominating thoughts and words *are* affirmations. It's important to recognize this, because we need to distinguish between these *naturally* occurring affirmations that drift in and out like the tides, and the conscious, thought-altering application of carefully conceived affirmations as a *process*.

Your *naturally* occurring thought/word affirmations just randomly do as they please—yet they're just as powerful as the affirmations *process* for turning intangibles into physical reality. If they team up with the Inner Critic to entrench whatever negative self-talk, worry, guilt and fear you happen to habitually indulge in, they can wash over you like a tidal wave and keep you engulfed in the circumstances you want out of.

Conversely, when you consciously put affirmations into practice as a *process,* and you combine it with other steps in this book, affirmations fling open the floodgates of positive change that can turn your life around.

> *Affirmations are like seed planted in soil.*
> *Poor soil, poor growth. Rich soil, abundant*
> *growth. The more you choose to think*

thoughts that make you feel good, the
quicker the affirmations work.
                                    –Louise L. Hay

The Case for Practicing
the Affirmations Process

The practice of affirmations has been given a bad rap by some. Even I, your Chief Affirmations Activist, thought the idea was pretty far out and silly when I first heard of it.

Some people arbitrarily assume it means mindlessly chanting empty words with the expectation of some magical result. So of course they conclude that the affirmations process can't possibly work. All I can say is, the naysayers either haven't tried it, or they haven't applied it as intended. There's too much evidence in the lives of real people—myself included—that the affirmations process not only works; it works big.

The affirmations process makes it possible for you to systematically create new ways of thinking, new fundamental beliefs, and a new foundational perspective—all of it leading to positive outcomes that can lift you out of your current circumstances and eventually change your life.

Creating affirmations is hands-down the best method of helping you think for your best good. It paves the straightest road to success—vigilance—by keeping you continuously aware of the everyday thoughts and words you're choosing. It trains your mind to challenge negative thoughts, words and beliefs *right on the spot* when they surface. It guides you to replace them with empowering, expansive thoughts of abundance until your voyage takes you all the way to the manifestation of your dreams as realities.

So of course the idea is to adopt affirmations as the premiere process for gaining control of your thoughts, your words, and yes, your destiny. Why wouldn't you? You already know that your dominating thoughts and words, repeated often enough and long enough, can become your reality. By consciously and routinely practicing the affirmations process, you can flip negative self-talk into positive statements that can become positive physical reality just as surely as negative ones will do the opposite.

In his book, *Think and Grow Rich*, Napoleon Hill wrote of countless successful people—rich and famous leaders with names that became household words—who practiced affirmations for the purpose of gaining wealth. In those days he called it "autosuggestion."

> *Recall what has been said about the subconscious mind resembling a fertile garden spot, in which weeds will grow in abundance, if the seeds of more desirable crops are not sown therein. AUTOSUGGESTION*

(affirming) is the agency of control through which an individual may voluntarily feed his subconscious mind on thoughts of a creative nature, or, by neglect, permit thoughts of a destructive nature to find their way into the rich garden of the mind.
                                              –Napoleon Hill

Others that have written extensively about affirmations include Louise L. Hay, Catherine Ponder, and Florence Scovel Shinn, the one who moved me most with her 1920s book, *The Game of Life and How to Play It.*

You will be a failure, until you impress the subconscious with the conviction you are a success. This is done by making an affirmation which "clicks."
                                      –Florence Scovel Shinn

Impress the subconscious. That's what affirmations do. By practicing affirmations repeatedly, and connecting them to your heart (Chapter Five), you're convincing your subconscious mind that your affirmation is true. This seems to choreograph the mysterious dance between the subconscious and the conscious mind that can eventually find you transforming your mental attitudes, habits, emotional reactions, behaviors and literally everything in your external world.

Our subconscious minds have no sense of humor, play no jokes and cannot tell the difference between reality and an imagined thought or image. What we continually think about eventually will manifest in our lives.

—Sidney Madwed

The Affirmations Process in a Nutshell

As most popularly taught, the affirmations process usually involves writing a short, positive, precisely worded statement in present tense describing a future outcome that you desire as if it has already come to be.

Once you've written your statement, you repeat it silently to yourself and out loud, over and over again, as often as you can. Eventually you'll think, speak, and affirm it into existence.

Only one thing registers on the subconscious mind: repetitive application— practice. What you practice is what you manifest.

—Fay Weldon

But wait. The process doesn't begin with your statement and its repetition. It goes hand-in-hand with every step in this book—especially creative visualization—to help you create desired outcomes in any area of your life.

Even before you write an affirmation, the process must have begun with your determination of who you are, what you want to Be, Do and Have, when you want it, and your decision to achieve it (Chapter One) ... combined with your belief that you can achieve it (Chapter Two) ... combined with your gloriously detailed visualization of having already achieved it (Chapter Three) ... combined with affirming it (this chapter) ... combined with connecting it to your heart (Chapter Five) ... combined with taking action to make it happen (Chapter Six) ... combined with being continuously grateful for what you have right now (Chapter Seven)! Yes! Just as these steps naturally intermingle as needed and can't be bound to any particular order, so does the practice of affirmations intertwine with them all throughout your journey. The point is that your understanding and performance of each and every step is essential for applying the affirmations process in a specific way.

> *Affirmation without discipline is the beginning of delusion.*
> –Jim Rohn

What I've experienced is this: once you have certitude about who you are, what you want, and a burning desire to get it, you have the beginnings of support for writing an effective affirmation. But keep on building from there. For example, maybe there's a really wide gap between where you are and where you want to be. And the Inner Critic rises up and says *Yeah right, that's never going to happen.* But by visualizing yourself having reached your destination, and by connecting that vision to your heart so you *feel* your desired outcome emotionally, you can narrow that gap and hold the Inner Critic at bay.

What's more, there's no point in speaking an affirmation without visualizing it as though it's occurring. Likewise, you can't say your affirmations in the morning and then think negatively all day. Visualization is meant to overpower negative thinking with a clear picture of the results you seek. And of course you're taking action all the while.

> *The vision that you glorify in your mind, the ideal that you have enthroned in your heart—this you will build your life by, and this you will become.*
>
> –James Allen

I feel that by bringing all the steps into play, all the forces of the universe combine to help me transform dreams into reality. Whatever I need in terms of people or circumstances, I will attract into my life. There is power in my intentions.

So we need the total package to reconstruct the way we think. Then we can create our affirmations with full intention, belief, desire and focus.

Five Principles for Writing Affirmations that Work

1. Write Affirmations in the Positive.

View your choice of words as the master key to creating positive change. Avoid words that describe something you *don't* want more of. For example, *don't* write "I am so happy and grateful that I am overcoming limitations and obstacles." *Do* write what you *do* want: "I am so happy and grateful that I am consistently growing and expanding."

> *Our subconscious minds only understand things in positive terms. If I say, 'Don't picture an elephant,' your mind will ignore the negative command and picture an elephant. Therefore, when you create your affirmations, choose only positive words that clearly and positively state what you want.*
>
> –Bill Marshall

2. Write Affirmations in the Present Tense.

Visualize yourself already in full possession of everything you're affirming. Then write the affirmation in the present tense. This influences your subconscious mind to accept that you've already achieved your goal, leaving no room there to believe otherwise, and tending to accelerate your progress. Own it now!

*Affirmation statements are going beyond
the reality of the present into the creation
of the future through the words you use in
the now.*
                                        –Louise L. Hay

3. Connect Your Affirmations to Your Heart.

Your heart is home to your emotions. Add genuine
emotion to your affirmations. You must feel the words
deeply, and infuse them with conviction and belief.
So choose those really juicy words that automatically
make your emotions go *Wow!*

*Remember, therefore, when reading aloud
the statement of your desire ... that the
mere reading of the words is of NO
CONSEQUENCE UNLESS you mix emotion, or
feeling, with your words.*
                                        –Napoleon Hill

4. Repeat Your Affirmations Silently and Aloud.

Repeat every word as often as you possibly can, but
at least once in the morning and once in the
evening.

*... repetition impresses the subconscious,
and we are then master of the situation.*
                                    –Florence Scovel Shinn

5. Make All of these Principles a Permanent Habit.

Practice all of these principles daily. Consistency is the key.

> *As long as you know what it is you desire, then by simply affirming that it is yours— firmly and positively, with no ifs, buts, or maybes—over and over again, from the minute you arise in the morning until the time you go to sleep at night, and as many times during the day as your work or activities permit, you will be drawn to those people, places, and events that will bring your desires to you.*
>
> –Scott Reed

TECHNIQUES FOR CREATING AND PRACTICING AFFIRMATIONS

I've been writing affirmations about every area of my life for many years now, and I know they really do work for achieving whatever I want to achieve. I've proven it countless times. And I've learned that as long as you stick to the five principles above, there are various ways to stylize your approach, your technique, your method of application. Let's look at a handful of these.

How to Get a Fast Start

An excellent way to get a fast start at writing affirmations is to begin them with the words "I am." This technique is so effective for impressing the subconscious mind that you can use it as a means to various ends.

You already have a head start. In Chapter One I asked you to use "I am" as a means of describing your life's mission and the qualities and character traits that you want to claim as your own. In Chapter Two you used "I am" to help examine your beliefs about several things. In Chapter Three you wrote an affirmation that began with the words "I am." The idea is to write "I am so happy and grateful now that I" or "I am so happy and grateful that I now" and then fill in the blank.

What to write in the blank? Since it's all about changing your current circumstances and creating new ones, just think of what you want to Be, Do and Have in any department of your life. I listed seven departments in Chapter One: Physical, Mental, Spiritual, Family/Friends/Relationships, Job/Career/Money, Adventure/Recreation, and Service/Contribution.

So for example, if you have a health issue, your affirmation for the Physical Department might go something like, "I am so happy and grateful now that my body is healthy, strong, resilient, and supports me in all I do." Remember that your affirmation must contain only what you do want, not what you don't want. For example, you wouldn't say you are now free of disease. Instead you'd say that you now have abundant health.

Or let's suppose you want to use the list of desirable qualities and character traits that you developed as a self-improvement goal for an exercise in Chapter One. When writing "I am" in front of each item on the list, you may have wound up with such affirmations as "I am courageous." "I am kind." "I am strong." "I am healthy." "I am a 'possibilities' thinker." And so on. Very powerful food for the subconscious mind.

You can also get a fast start by creating an "I am" affirmation around the question, "What is the most empowering thing I could believe about _____?"

Looking back at the exercises in Chapter Two, you'll see that the word "money" was an option. So now you'd want to write an affirmation that goes "I am so happy and grateful that money now comes to me abundantly, rapidly and with ease from multiple expected and unexpected sources. Everywhere I turn, money flows to me. I give thanks." Notice that "Everywhere I turn" adds emotion to the affirmation; and you've also added gratitude. For more specificity if you depend on customers or clients for your income, you might add something like "My ideal clients (or customers) are running to me now."

Using "I am" will always lock you into the necessity of writing affirmations in present tense. Before I was big into affirmations I was thinking, *I want to write a book.* The thought was so precious and seemed so unattainable that I couldn't even get the words out of my mouth to tell someone. Had I known then what I know now about affirmations, I wouldn't have been thinking *I want to write a book.* I would have created a bold affirmation claiming it, like "I am so happy and grateful that my first book has been published and is positively impacting countless lives." Needless to say, I eventually wrote that affirmation, repeated it over and over again, took action, and my dream became reality.

Just remember that the words "I am" have such a profound influence on the subconscious that you must be careful when choosing the words to follow them. They will be the most important words in your vocabulary because the "I am" portends your destiny.

A Systematic Formula for Daily Affirmations Practice

This is a formula you would practice every day for as many weeks as it takes to get the results you want. My daughter Ashley started using it with amazing results during her first year at Chapman University.

Make a list of either 7, 14 or 21 things you want to accomplish. Write an affirmation about each one. If you write seven, repeat one per day per week. If you write 14, repeat 2 per day per week. Ashley wrote 21, so that meant repeating 3 per day per week.

She established a morning practice of repeating her three affirmations over and over in her mind and out loud for 10 to 15 minutes. Eventually she memorized them all, and this fixed them clearly on her radar. As I write this she has continued to keep it up with remarkable discipline.

In the beginning there was a wide gap between where she was and the achievement of some of those 21 goals. She said there were times she'd say *Oh this is just bull,* but she kept at it. Already she has closed the gap on several fronts. For one thing she's been getting straight A grades.

One of her goals was to create a book about smiling through life. We wrote an affirmation that said "I am so happy and grateful for the inspiration that flows through me daily for my smile book. I stay open to insights that come from all sources to aid in the completion of this book by this Christmas."

Ashley composed affirmations about creating a movement around her book. One day she was amazed to find that out of the blue, she was meeting people with exactly the right talents to help her advance that goal. One was a graphic design student who needed a project for her major, so she created Ashley's website. Another was a media student who needed a video project, so she made a video around Ashley's idea of the smile campaign. Eventually she even met some highly accomplished, high-priced people outside of college who gave freely of their consulting time to the project.

I have so many similar examples in my own experience that I'm convinced Ashley attracted those resources due to her consistent practice of affirmations, staying open, and taking the right consistent actions.

Recording Audio Affirmations in Your Voice

Several years ago I started using an affirmation software program to record and play back my affirmations in my own voice. I would record them when I felt in a place of clarity and power and purpose, so when I listened to them I could recapture the same feeling of conviction that is so needed to impress the subconscious mind. And I could add a musical background to amplify the sense of passion that makes affirmations even more potent.

The results were amazing. I noticed how much faster my progress was with every goal. And not only that. Something about this method found me setting more and more goals—especially those that are such a big deal and seemingly so distant that I almost dared not even voice them. Still, when I recorded them and played them back over and over again I was seeing some of them come into reality in as little as a month!

The Importance of Being Specific

I can think of so many things I've wanted that came into being after I learned the importance of using very specific language in my affirmations.

A few years ago, I decided it was time to find my man. I'd been single for seven years. My kids were becoming adults, and very involved in their own lives.

I wrote an affirmation that was very bold and specific. Notice that I didn't ask for anything that I wasn't willing to give in return. It read,

> *I am attracting men who are single, emotionally available, financially stable and free, open, honest, intuitive, communicative, sensitive, spiritual, intelligent, funny, balanced, healthy, tender and loving—and who encourage, support and help me to be, do and have all that is my destiny—as I bring all of the same to them.*

I spoke it out loud to some friends. "Good luck finding *that*," said they.

But guess what. I gave it a deadline—the end of the coming December—and on November 16th, I met my fiancé. Ray is everything I wanted, and even more than I could have hoped for.

Affirmations work.

Add Gratefulness

Include a sprinkle of gratitude in your collection of affirmations. Here's a little example: "I now live with a grateful heart and see my life's many gifts through eyes of childlike wonder."

The Finish

An excellent way to end any affirmation statement is with the words of Shakti Gawain: "This or something better now manifests for me in totally satisfying and harmonious ways, for the highest good of all concerned."

AFFIRMATIONS YOU CAN USE FOR EACH STEP IN THIS BOOK

Affirmations for "Decide What You Want"

1. I am following a clear and definite process to manifest my desires into physical reality.
2. I am now sending a clear message of what I desire.
3. I now make clear and committed decisions of exactly what I want.
4. I now make decisions that align with my life's purpose and highest values.
5. I now make definite decisions, and follow through with immediate and specific results-focused action.
6. I now make a definite decision, and the unseen forces of the universe move to help me manifest it into reality.

7. I now boldly express the natural gifts I was born with.

WRITE TWO OF YOUR OWN HERE

_____

_____

_____

_____

_____

Affirmations for "Build Belief"

1. I consciously choose my beliefs.
2. I am now moving forward with a feeling of absolute certainty that I can and will achieve my goals.
3. I have a clear understanding of my beliefs. I give my focus and energy only to beliefs that support my highest good.
4. I now know that I deserve the best that life has to offer, and the best is flowing into my life.
5. I now have all of the resources and talent I need to achieve my goals.
6. I am a limitless being. All that I need to achieve my dreams is within me now or will be provided.
7. I only choose beliefs that empower me.

WRITE TWO OF YOUR OWN HERE

_____

_____

_____

_____

_____

_____

Affirmations for
"Craft a Compelling Vision"

1. I dream lofty dreams. My dreams are becoming my everyday reality.
2. My vision is the promise of who I am becoming.
3. I create big, bold, and bright pictures in my mind of myself enjoying the realization of my desires.
4. The mental pictures I create are clear and specific.
5. I set big and grand goals. My desire to achieve my big goals energizes and empowers me to consistently grow and expand.
6. I have a clear Definite Major Purpose.
7. I am a creator. I hold onto the clear pictures of what I desire until I create the reality.

8. I have a detailed vision of what I want to Be, Do, and Have.

9. I create vision boards to help me clarify my vision and I review them daily with a feeling of certainty.

WRITE TWO OF YOUR OWN HERE

_____

_____

_____

_____

_____

_____

Affirmations for
"Think It, Speak It, Affirm It Into Existence"

1. I regularly engage in creative brainstorming. I freely explore ideas without knowing exactly where they will lead.

2. My inner dialog is working for me.

3. I monitor my thoughts. I choose thought habits that encourage and support me.

4. I create powerful affirmations in present tense that help me stay focused on what I want.

5. I record my affirmations and listen to them over and over again.

6. I use the power of positive thought to create positive lasting change.

7. My power affirmations are changing my reality.

WRITE TWO OF YOUR OWN HERE

_____

_____

_____

_____

_____

_____

Affirmations for
"Connect to the Heart"

1. I am pursuing my heart's desires.
2. I create from my head and my heart.
3. I build positive emotion around my desires.
4. I imagine the objects of my desires in my possession in advance.
5. I now animate my goals and dreams with the feelings of my heart.
6. I now readily forgive myself and others.
7. I now keep my heart space open and free.

WRITE TWO OF YOUR OWN HERE

_____

_____

_____

_____

Affirmations for "Act"

1. I am starting right now to move towards the achievement of my goals.
2. I take action towards my goals every day.
3. I now take quick and courageous action.
4. I move towards solutions with massive results-focused action.
5. I am willing to begin where I am right now, and learn and grow as I go.
6. I know that everything counts. I celebrate all progress, large or small, towards my goals.
7. I always put forth my best effort in everything I do.
8. I am so grateful that I have now achieved my goals and am enjoying the fruits of my efforts.

WRITE TWO OF YOUR OWN HERE

CHAPTER FIVE

Step Five
Connect with the Heart

So let your deepest desires direct your aim. Set your sights far above the "reasonable" target. The power of purpose is profound only if you have a desire that stirs the heart.

–Price Pritchett

If you're like most people, you probably spend more time in your head than in your heart just to keep pace with the dynamics of daily life. And the steps described so far have been about work to be done in your head. By taking these steps and all exercises, you have

- searched your depths for your Definite Major Purpose;
- identified your purpose in life and exactly what you want;
- decided you're going to get it;
- built the belief that you will get it;
- crafted your vision of it;

- started the process of thinking, speaking, and affirming your goal into existence; and
- learned ways to control your Inner Voice so your thinking won't sabotage you.

Congratulations again! You've made tremendous progress. Now let's connect to the heart.

What do I mean by this?

When people say they're looking for meaning in life, what they're really seeking is a deep experience. We all want an experience so deep that we seem to literally "feel" it filling the heart. To the brim and running over.

Exercise 5-1:
An Experience
that Filled My Heart

Think of a time when something profoundly wonderful happened to you. Something or someone you wanted finally came into your life. Whatever "it" was, "it" stirred your emotions so deeply that "it" leapt into your heart and filled it to the brim. Write that event down right here in, say, 25 words or so.

_____

_____

_____

_____

Remember how full you felt in the very center of your chest when that happened? *That's* how I want you to feel about whatever goal you're pursuing. Right now, before you reach it. Just as you've learned to visualize yourself achieving your goal and celebrating it in your mind's eye before you get there, now you need to start "living" your vision in your heart.

Please visit
http://www.absolutelyanythingyouwant.com to
download printable PDF copies of this exercise.

All of the great teachers who show us how to write, read, visualize and affirm a goal always add that you've got to get your deepest, most positive emotions involved. Why?

When you begin with a wisp of an idea and grow it through the creative process of decision-making, believing and envisioning, you're constructing a foundation of mental clarity. This is every bit as essential as the foundation of a skyscraper. But at this stage your idea still consists of empty pictures, empty words, and wishes. You don't begin to securely grasp your idea, your decision, your belief, your dream until it descends from your mind to your heart. Now your dream becomes infused with power. You feel it. You fall in love with it. And according to popular belief, it's not until you "feel things in your heart" that they can truly be on their way to you.

Of course, I subscribe to this belief because the evidence abounds in the success stories of people everywhere. Certainly I've arrived at this "full heart" phenomenon many times while evolving through the six steps in this book. For example I'm thinking of the time when I first decided that I wanted a second home in San Diego so I could be close to my grown children.

The thought arrived in the typical wrappings of worry, doubt and fear. All the usual maddening back-and-forth arguments persisted in my head for a painfully long time. When I couldn't stand it any longer, I just put my foot down and said "I can make this happen!"

So that was the decision point. I had various affirmations around it and such, but it wasn't until the idea descended into my heart that it began to manifest. I believe it descended when I overwhelmed the Inner Critic with an affirmation that said, "I am so happy and grateful that I am waking up in the morning in San Diego ... that I can feel and smell the ocean breeze ... that I can pick up the phone and call my children and be at lunch with any of them in less than 30 minutes."

When I got into that place, the pace picked up around my dream.

And it did become reality. In exactly the right way and at exactly the right time.

The Pivotal Point in Your Journey

You have to connect with the heart. This is the pivotal point in your journey toward whatever you want. This is when your dream begins to gather density. It takes on a certain substance. It builds a certain momentum. You're not just thinking or visualizing what you want; you're actually starting to feel it. In this part of the creative process you are bringing your dream *that close* to the precious moment when it physically shows up in your life.

You see, your deepest, most positive emotions—joy, peace, love—virtually reside in "the heart of you." Call it your spiritual heart if you will. It's where we seem to hold and experience harmony with the universe, the world, and life in all its forms. But it can also hold your deepest, most negative emotions. And by expressing the feelings you "feel in your heart," you are sending messages that the world mirrors back to you, for better or for worse. And so, it's what you feel in your heart that either attracts more negativity to you, or *animates your dreams and brings them to you faster!*

What you focus on with thought and feeling
is what you attract into your experience,
whether or not it's something you want.
                                        –Bob Doyle

So how do you connect your dream from your head to your heart? Like a fabulous meal, it's all in the preparation.

- Clear the pathway. Build positive emotion around your desires—Be, Do, Have—and imagine yourself in possession of them right now.
- Notice, intensify and expand the passion, commitment, excitement and joy that you feel around your goals and affirmations.
- Celebrate it even before you have it.
- Be grateful every day for what you have right now.
- Make space in your heart for these feelings by getting rid of the heart closers: the toxic, negative emotions that have crept in over the years or even in the last few minutes.

Don't underestimate the power of living with an open heart and engaging your emotions for creating anything of value. When you keep the heart space open and unencumbered by past and future distractions, here's what happens:

- You are free to totally feel the feelings that support the outcome you desire.
- You can bring to bear your creative forces for living in the present moment and drawing what you want from the world.
- The world will mirror back the good that radiates from you.

Begin now by recognizing and getting rid of the heart closers so you can stay open to every possible providence that could come your way through other people.

> Just let the golden, beautiful, powerful, creative nature that you are, flow unobstructed.
>
> –Hale Dwoskin

HEART CLOSERS

There are certain things that shut us down. They just shut us down. We can't think clearly, and we can't bring our desired resources and relationships into being, if we're shut down in the heart.

Heart closers may emerge when you first react to whatever people say or do that hurts or upsets you. You can feel heart closers in your body. Left to do their damage, they make you rigid and they can make you sick. They latch onto you like parasites and won't let go unless you take the initiative to get rid of them. If you don't, they remain attached to you. And you become attached to them! This alliance promotes their growth into all sorts of negative forms: anger, resentment, jealousy, grudge-bearing, blame-passing, defensiveness, criticism, chronic complaining, self-righteousness, vengefulness ... on and on and on. And the good news is, for every heart closer, there's a heart opener.

HEART OPENERS

It all begins with love. While heart openers can be described as many qualities, attitudes and behaviors—forgiveness, tolerance, compassion, kindness, just to name a few—every one of them is a manifestation of love. Love is their very wellspring.

> *There is no difficulty that enough love will not conquer ... no door that enough love will not open, no gulf that enough love will not bridge, no wall that enough love will not throw down. It makes no difference how deeply seated may be the trouble; how hopeless the outlook; how muddled the tangle; how great the mistake. A sufficient realization of love will dissolve it all. If only you could love enough you would be the happiest and most powerful being in the world ...*
>
> —Emmet Fox

But love must flow from you to *you* before it can flow to others. Then, you become a magnet. A powerful, powerful magnet that people are drawn to. One that makes others feel good. Miracles will unfold if you stay open to that reality.

> *Anything that makes you feel good is always going to be drawing in more.*
> —Dr. John Gray

Loving Yourself

You and I and all of us are infinitely connected with all of life. And the world around you is your mirror, reflecting how you feel about yourself. Just as a smile attracts a smile, so does the love you give to yourself extend to others, inspiring them to love you back. It's so simple.

> *There's something so magnificent about you. And as you love yourself, you'll love others.*
> —Bob Proctor

Loving yourself is at once easy and hard. Oh, it's so easy when you're at the top of your game, isn't it. And it's so hard when you mess up, isn't it. When you feel engulfed in disapproval, when you feel displaced or lost, when you have zero inspiration or drive, it seems a stretch to even think that you could possibly love yourself! But you must. Whatever the circumstances, you need to give love to yourself through all the ups and downs.

Sometimes it takes so little to make loving ourselves so hard. Years ago I put on a fabulous event that brought rave reviews from scores of people saying how beneficial, how touching, how life-changing it was. Then one person made a slightly critical remark—and what do you think I took home? Of course. It was that one negative comment.

Later that night I was still holding onto that one comment. All the kudos had sort of just bounced off of me while this one negative comment got in and stuck. Crazy, I said to myself, because I knew I had nailed it. I knew I had done a great job.

So I did a little evening exercise. I scanned back through the day. I thought of the joy and tears in peoples' eyes, the warm hugs and the excitement, and the sense of accomplishment and satisfaction that I felt. And I just decided to give all the weight to those emotions and feelings. By immersing myself in that picture, I was finally able to release this one little critical comment that someone made.

We tend to internalize a negative comment so much more readily than a positive one that we forget to give ourselves credit for what we've done right, much less celebrate it. We jump all over ourselves if we make a mistake or if someone says something negative. We're way too tough on ourselves. I think most people suffer with this challenge to one degree or another.

So of course, the solution is to focus on what you do right.

Exercise 5-2
What Did I Do Right Today?

Acknowledge and celebrate your achievements as they occur throughout the day. Tonight, open this book to this page, and write them down. Then start a diary dedicated to just this one question, and enter your answer every night.

_____

_____

_____

_____

_____

_____

_____

_____

_____

_____

Please visit
http://www.absolutelyanythingyouwant.com to download printable PDF copies of this exercise.

Be your own best cheerleader! Give yourself the gift of being the most enthusiastic, supportive person in your life! You might be one of those people who loves and forgives others freely without ever extending the same gifts to yourself. Give yourself those gifts. Realize that this can only deepen and enhance your ability to love and forgive others.

Quit punishing yourself. Don't hold on to your mistakes. Let them go.

When I feel that I haven't done my best and I start beating myself up, I turn my thoughts to how I would treat a young child if she were in my situation. I would encourage her. I would pick her up and hug her and say "good job!" Then I think of myself as that child. Think of yourself as that child. You're never too old to give yourself the love and reassurance craved by adults and children alike. I'll bet that when you give this gift to yourself, you'll be surprised how many more gifts come into your life from the outside.

> *Go for the sense of inner joy, of inner peace, of inner vision first and then all the other things from the outside appear.*
> —Marci Shimoff

Forgiving Yourself and Others

Forgiveness begins with love. Love for yourself and others. Forgiveness is about honoring yourself and others. Accepting yourself and others. Opening your heart to yourself and others. And freeing yourself from the pain in your past so you can live fully in the present. Forgiveness is about peace. Forgiveness is essential to your health.

Begin by simply forgiving yourself for being human! After all, as a human, you're imperfect! We all are. So just accept that.

Look. None of the opportunities to learn and contribute and evolve would be presented to you by this life if you had already perfected every aspect of your being. So cut some slack for yourself and others. Here, take this simple affirmation. Put it to work on forgiving yourself starting now:

> I completely love, forgive and accept myself. I now give myself the perfect nurturing I long for.

And then get to work on your feelings toward others.

Anger, resentments, harsh judgments, grudges—all the unforgiven things we carry around inside—they brew, they fester, they cause incredible pain. They are literally toxic.

I've seen people age almost overnight as a result of hanging onto resentment.

I've seen people gain weight from feeding on the grievances in their hearts.

I've seen anger grip people so tightly that they come to a standstill in life's journey.

Conversely I've seen forgiveness melt away these bitter feelings. I've seen healing, beautiful healing, and unspeakable joy and peace flow into people's lives when their toxic burdens were lifted.

If anything, I've learned that I forgive too easily. Seeing many sides of an issue, I can almost justify the position of even those who may have seriously wronged me. But forgiving others doesn't mean you just blindly take their abuse. Nor does it mean repeatedly putting yourself into situations that cause you pain.

I'm not encouraging you to be a doormat.

I'm not saying you must be such a positive person that you can put a positive spin on any negatives that come your way.

I *am* saying there's a fine balance between noticing the hurt, deciding what to do, course-correcting and then releasing it.

I *am* saying the cool thing about forgiveness is that it's wide open to choice. In this respect it's no different from any other attitude or belief. You can *choose* to forgive. And you can choose to do so either by simply unplugging, or by analyzing and working through the problem in detail until you get closure.

The "Simply Unplug" Method of Forgiveness

As described in Chapter Four, we use the "unplug" method to stop talking to ourselves about whatever worries us. Now let's apply it to forgiveness. In this case you're just flat-out refusing to allow a person's words or actions to hurt you, worry you, eat up your time, sap your energy, linger and lurk, and take up the heart space you need for productive emotions. So unplugging works great as the fastest, most straightforward way to forgive and create closure for a grievance.

I'm not suggesting that you use this method to just gloss over the grievance, or that you suppress your feelings about it, or that you go into denial of it. I'm saying you need to be fully aware of the problem when it occurs, and you need to acknowledge your feelings about it before you can successfully pull the plug. Otherwise, any feelings you suppress will keep bubbling up as anger, resentment, bitterness, blaming, complaining and on and on; and one day they could show up as some disorder or dis-ease in your body.

As such, the unplug method requires you to have a full grasp of your feelings while bypassing the heavy detail. You don't need to analyze or fully understand all the whats, hows and whys of the situation. You don't need to own the event. You don't even need to say the forgivee is right. You just acknowledge the problem's presence, and then let it go. Drop it. Unplug. Replace it with a bigger thought. A bigger idea. A worthy idea.

A great way to conclude this method of forgiving is to say in your heart to the other party, "I send you love." Even if it makes no sense to you, just repeat the words, "I send you love. I unplug. I send you love."

Ho'o Pono Pono

I learned an even more abbreviated forgiveness technique when interviewing the best-selling author, Marci Shimoff. She told me she had seen miracles happen when using the ancient Hawaiian Kahuna practice of Ho'o pono pono. It consists of no more than saying these four short phrases to yourself and feeling them in your heart toward anyone you're holding a grudge against, including yourself.

**I'm sorry. Please forgive me.
Thank you. I love you.**

How sweet is its simplicity.

Marci explained that she and her sister had once had such a terrible argument that they stopped speaking to each other. Months later, when meeting for the first time at a family gathering, they couldn't even make eye contact.

Marci finally went to her car and practiced Ho'o pono pono for ten minutes. She said her heart just melted and she felt great compassion. She went back inside without saying a word and within minutes, her sister reached for her hand. Marci told me that this marked a huge shift in their relationship.

Three months later, their mother passed away. Marci realized how awful it would have been if she and her sister had still been estranged when returning to their mother's home to settle her estate.

> *When you forgive, you heal your own anger*
> *and hurt and are able to let love lead again.*
> *It's like spring cleaning for your heart.*
> —Marci Shimoff

Exercise 5-3
Five Situations Requiring
Forgiveness and Closure

Give Ho'o pono pono a try. Write down five situations where you're still harboring some resentment and need to replace it with forgiveness for anyone including yourself. Then for each of these situations during the next 24 hours, repeat "I'm sorry. Please forgive me. Thank you. I love you." Watch the anger dissipate and the situation shift based on your

STEP FIVE: CONNECT WITH THE HEART   173

intention to heal it. Practice Ho'o pono pono and see what shows up in your life!

1. _____

_____

_____

_____

2. _____

_____

_____

3. _____

_____

_____

_____

4. _____

_____

_____

_____

5. _____

_____

_____

_____

Please visit
http://www.absolutelyanythingyouwant.com to
download printable PDF copies of this exercise.

The "Analyze and Work It Through" Method of Forgiveness

Start this method by identifying and dissecting the grievance.

- What happened, exactly?
- What were the emotions?
- Where exactly is the hurt?
- Why does it hurt?
- What are you saying to yourself about it?
- Why do these issues keep popping up?
- What might you have done to attract this?
- What could you have done differently?
- What can you learn?

Take as much ownership of the situation as you can. Then ...

- What do you think must happen in order to finish this unfinished business?
- Do you want a conversation?
- Do you want an apology?
- Do you want to apologize?
- Should you write a letter?
- Or is it something you can just unplug from?

Before taking any action, you've got to break the grip of your emotions. You must fully feel them so you can then let them go. And you have to let them go. Give yourself permission to feel them, every one. Open your heart to all of life, and all that life holds for you. Let rigidity dissolve. Let yourself be angry. Let yourself be sad. Shed some tears if you want to.

Allowing yourself to feel anger doesn't mean that you have permission to rage or hurt anyone. It means getting the anger out of your system for the sake of your health, and so you can feel centered, grounded and able to approach a solution in a rational way. If your emotions have reached the boiling point, most likely your ego is taking over and you're developing some righteousness—a stubborn conviction that you're right—about whatever is going on. You have to turn the boiling down to a simmer until you can get the ego out of the way.

Some people get rid of their emotions by venting all their anger in writing until it's completely diffused. Psychologists call this "written catharsis" and it's so effective a cleanser that they recommend it as a matter of routine. It becomes the letter that you write but never send to the forgivee. It's strictly for your own detoxification, and it works.

If you decide to contact the forgivee, maybe a simple phone conversation will do. Or if you decide to do it by letter, clearly write what you understand about the problem, and add your love and forgiveness.

Nothing is good or bad, but thinking makes it so.

—William Shakespeare

However you do it, take action. Get rid of your emotions, forgive, make space in your heart for the good stuff, and move on.

And if you're feeling stuck after trying several strategies, I highly recommend diving into *The Work of Byron Katie.* Consisting of four questions and a turnaround, it's a simple yet profound method for achieving forgiveness. I've seen people that had been trapped for years in the grip of unforgiving bitterness just *let it all go* in 20 or 30 minutes at her seminars.

Honoring Yourself and Others

When you honor and respect yourself and others, you are growing the flowers of love and compassion. They bloom brightly and spread their fertile seeds over weed-infested fields of heart closers. The common names of these heart closers include Self-Righteousness, Rushing to Judgment, Blame-Passing, Unfair Criticism and Chronic Complaining.

Honor yourself for your thoughts, your feelings, your responses and your deeds. Honor yourself by choosing the highest and best way; by reaching for the best that's in you.

Honor others by assuming that they too are striving for the highest and best way, and doing the best they can. Remember that we're all connected. Give people the benefit of the doubt instead of arbitrarily drawing conclusions about them when you don't have all the facts. You don't know all the details of their lives. Even if you did, it's not your place to judge them. Keep this concept in mind during all communications. It will shine through even to those who are living and behaving on a lower plane, and it can sometimes inspire them to lift themselves higher. Be the one to hold the higher ground—the bigger space—and you'll see how people ultimately step into it.

Look at this email that came my way. It's about compassion and I think this says it all:

> *Dear God help us remember that the jerk who cut us off in traffic last night is a single mom who worked nine hours that day and was rushing home to cook dinner, help with homework, do the laundry, and spend a few precious minutes with her children.*

> *Help us to remember that that pierced tattoo disinterested young man, who can't seem to make change correctly, is a worried 19-year-old college student balancing his apprehension over his final exams with a fear of not getting his student loan for next semester.*

*Let us remember Lord that that scary look-
ing bum begging for money at the same
spot every day that really ought to get a job
is a slave to addictions that we can only
imagine in our worst nightmares.*

*Help us to remember that the old couple
walking annoyingly slow through the store
aisles and blocking our shopping progress,
are savoring this moment knowing that
based on a biopsy report she got back last
week this will be their last shared shopping
together.*

*Dear God, remind us each day, that of all of
the gifts you give us, the greatest is love. It
is not enough to share that love with those
we hold dear, or open our hearts just to
those who are close to us, but to all
humanity.*

*Let us be slow to judge and quick to for-
give, and show patience, empathy and love.
And the sum total of all of our lives and the
only thing that really matters when all is
said and done, is how much we love and
how much we're loved in return.*

And yet, some people would rather be right than
be loved. By nature, we all think we're right most of
the time. And the need to be right can get out of
hand. When you find yourself needing to be right and

you get all worked up, you can be sure that your ego has taken over and that you're in danger of becoming self-righteous. You can't create peace and unity from that place. You only isolate yourself and dissipate your energy. Carlos Casteneda wrote about the energy we waste just holding up our own importance, and that "You will never feel better about yourself by making others look worse."

So keep your need to be right in check. If you have a choice between being right and being kind, choose kind.

Being Kind

I was in Shavasana, the final yoga pose, and it had been a really good class. My heart was very open and tender. Our teacher simply said in this beautiful and sweet and humble voice, "Be kind to each other, Namaste."

What simple words. Honor yourself as you go about your day. Be kind to each other. And it just struck me, if we could only keep that simple idea in mind. Just be in tune and keep our hearts open to the people around us wherever we go. The checker ringing up the groceries, the server in the restaurant, the people on a busy street or in a store or airport— wherever, don't miss a chance to be kind.

I make it a point to smile and send love through my eyes, or give a little word, a little praise, a genuine compliment in these brief encounters with strangers everywhere. It helps me keep my heart open, and maybe it helps them in some small way too. It's one more way—such an easy and simple way—to celebrate life, be joyful, and radiate love and happiness. Don't miss the chance. Don't miss the chance.

> *Carpe Diem! Rejoice while you are alive; live the day; live life to the fullest; make the most of what you have. It is later than you think.*
> —Quintus Horatius Flaccus, aka Horace

Carpe Diem is Latin for "seize the day." Seize every opportunity to make someone's day. Leave a trail of random acts of kindness in your wake. In the grocery store, let someone get in line ahead of you. On the road, pay the toll for the driver behind you. When you put a smile on someone's face and he receives it gratefully, who knows where it ripples out from there. I mean, why not? We're occupying this space together, here on Earth. Make their day! Don't miss the chance.

> *I've learned that people will forget what you said. People will forget what you did, but people will never forget how you made them feel.*
> —Maya Angelou

Taming the Fox

One of my favorite books is *The Little Prince* by the French author Antoine de Saint-Exupery. It's a children's book but it's filled with deeper messages and beautiful analogies about relationships and life themes.

In the story, a beautiful process unfolds where the Little Prince tames a fox. They become great friends by observing certain rites, and they gradually gain each other's trust.

When it's time for them to part their ways and say goodbye, the fox is very sad and begins crying. The Little Prince says, "Come here. I have a secret for you. Here is my secret; it is quite simple. It is only with the heart that one can see rightly. What is essential is invisible to the eye."

Whenever I find myself in an uncomfortable place with someone, I think of taming the fox. I associate this "taming" with being kind to others and exerting some simple effort to add positively to their lives. One such opportunity presents itself every time I fly to San Diego.

My home in San Diego is such a short cab ride from the airport that it's hardly worth it to the driver. They need bigger fares because they have to pay a fee every time they enter the airport. So my cab rides always begin with "I'm so sorry!" when I give them the nearby address. Last time the response was "Ohh, okay," from a crestfallen driver.

I could have gone all defensive and said something like, "Well, I gotta take somebody's cab, don't I? I mean what am I gonna to do? I gotta get there, and like, isn't this is your job?" And then we'd have to ride together in uneasy silence while our energies drained away. So I decided that I'd rather tame the fox. I had seven or eight minutes to turn the energy in that cab around.

I asked him, "What are your airport fees?" After answering, he said he had wanted just one more big fare so he could go get his oil changed and knock off for the day.

I got the message. I commiserated with him a little, and then gradually shifted to other topics. His family, my family, where he came from, what he likes about being here, and within four or five minutes we were engaged in laughter together. It was genuine. I could just feel his heart open up. My spirits were lifted too. With just a little effort I had completely changed that driver's state of mind. I felt I had made his day, even before tipping him double the fare.

> *Beginning today, treat everyone you meet as if they were going to be dead by midnight. Extend to them all the care, kindness, and understanding you can muster, and do it with no thought of any reward. Your life will never be the same again.*
>
> —Og Mandino

Asking

There's one heart opener that I suspect is especially hard for most people. It certainly was hard for me in days gone by. It's about being able to open your heart so wide that you can open your mouth and ask for what you want.

I spent many years as a one woman band, being so performance-driven and so willing to lead that I wouldn't lean on anyone for anything. I just moved forward with dogged determination and rarely consulted anyone about any decision I made. But during the last several years I've come to realize what an incredible resource I have around me—people that know and understand things I'll never know and understand. I've learned the importance of masterminding, and have gained a great deal from my mastermind groups in the last few years. Now I regularly ask people for help, advice and input, and I value their additional perspectives.

I now realize that no one creates huge success solo. If your heart is closed to input from others and you never ask, you may indeed find it harder to ultimately get what you want. As W. Clement Stone put it, "If there is something to gain and nothing to lose by asking, by all means ask!"

This must be why the brilliant success coach Jack Canfield teaches "asking" in his seminars. When I interviewed him for one of my telesummits, he said, "In my seminars I teach people to ask ask ask ask ask ask." He went on to explain that if you don't ask, you won't get anything anyway, so why not ask for the things you want and need? You have nothing to lose.

> *People who ask confidently get more than those who are hesitant and uncertain. When you've figured out what you want to ask for, do it with certainty, boldness and confidence.*
>
> –Jack Canfield

And so, invite people in. Open your heart and let people in so you can benefit from the richness of their experience. You'll be surprised how many people are eager to help and advise and be a part of your creative process. It makes them feel valued. It makes them feel good. It's one more way to love and be loved in return.

> *Everything you want out there is waiting for you to ask. Everything you want also wants you. But you have to take action to get it.*
>
> –Jules Renard

Blessing It

Do you want something so badly that you find yourself feeling jealous when others have it and you don't? You must know what a heart closer it is to compare yourself with others. It just makes you feel awful and it shuts people out of your life.

Author-speaker T. Harv Eker teaches that whenever we see something we want that belongs to some-
body else, we must bless it. I think this is right on. If
you want a fabulous home, don't be jealous of those
who own one. Don't resent them or say negative
things about them. Bless their home. Acknowledge it
and return to your dreams and desires. This keeps
your heart open so you can keep connecting your
dreams from your mind to your heart until you can
bring your dreams to reality. One more time, it's all
about love.

Giving to Receive

Whatever you want to bring into your life, you must
give it. If you want love, understanding, abundance,
appreciation, joy, happiness, whatever it is—you need
to give it to someone. That means giving something to
someone all the time, doesn't it! Because you want
these things for yourself all the time, don't you!

When I was a little girl I thought my great
grandma Hodell was onto some special secret. She was
a German immigrant and quite poor by ordinary standards. She just radiated joy and love and peace and
happiness even when she was ill. It had to be due to
this beautiful giving attitude that she had toward
others. Her way of giving was to bake a cake for a
neighbor whenever she didn't feel well.

How simple, yet how profound. By turning her
attention away from herself to create and give a labor

of love, she received everything back from everyone whose spirits she had lifted.

> *Take time off to give to yourself, in a sense to fill yourself up to fullness, to where now you can overflow in giving.*
> —Dr. John Gray

Thinking Young

Living with an open heart keeps you young. As you move into a new day, you're not jaded by the past. You have an adventurous, curious attitude. You see the world around you with wonder and awe. Nothing expresses this more clearly than this quotation that I gave to my paternal grandmother, my Nana Marjorie Christiansen, when she was in her twilight years:

Youth

> *Youth is not a time of life. It is a state of mind. It is not a matter of red cheeks, red lips and supple knees. It is a temper of the will; a quality of the imagination; a vigor of the emotions; it is a freshness of the deep springs of life.*

> *Youth means a temperamental predominance of courage over timidity, of the appetite for adventure over a life of ease. This often exists in a man of fifty, more than in a boy of twenty. Nobody grows old by merely*

living a number of years; people grow old by deserting their ideals.

Years may wrinkle the skin, but to give up enthusiasm wrinkles the soul. Worry, doubt, self-distrust, fear and despair— these are the long, long years that bow the head and turn the growing spirit back to dust.

Whether seventy or sixteen, there is in every being's heart a love of wonder; the sweet amazement at the stars and starlike things and thoughts; the undaunted challenge of events, the unfailing childlike appetite for what comes next, and the joy in the game of life.

You are as young as your faith, as old as your doubt; as young as your self-confidence, as old as your fear; as young as your hope, as old as your despair.
                                   –Samuel Ullman

My Nana always had that youthful spirit about her. Remembering how vital she was in her golden years, romping with my kids on the floor and playing with water balloons—and how she still lived in this beautiful state of awe during her 90s—I can only conclude that her profound sense of wonder, amazement and gratefulness kept her youthful to the end.

I tucked the same poem into a birthday card for my mom when she turned 75. She too continues to carry in her heart "a love of wonder; the sweet amazement at the stars and starlike things and thoughts; the undaunted challenge of events, the unfailing childlike appetite for what comes next, and the joy in the game of life." No wonder she still has that young girl's sparkle in her eyes and a level of energy that few can keep up with.

I'm so grateful to have had a lifetime in the presence of such remarkable women.

Living Life
With a Grateful Heart

Living in a state of gratefulness is perhaps the most powerful heart opener there is. And as you've seen, back in Chapter One I made gratefulness a must for you.

In his book, *Gratefulness, the Heart of Prayer*, Brother David Steindl-Rast speaks of the heart as the "whole person," and gratefulness as a "full response." He says our whole person is engaged when we're grateful.

"When we reach our innermost heart," he writes, "we reach a realm where we are not only intimately at home with ourselves, but intimately united with others, all others. The heart is not a lonely place. It is the realm where solitude and togetherness coincide."

He describes gratefulness as full aliveness, and aliveness as the symbol of the heart.

He writes of the mother who sees her sleeping infant through the same eyes every afternoon, but who one day sees the same scene through the eyes of her heart, and "her whole heart is filled with gratefulness too deep for words." Such moments of the heart involve a "deep, all-pervading, overflowing sense of gratefulness" and it is not the same as thanksgiving. We'll explore this idea further in Chapter Seven. Suffice it to say, living life with a grateful heart for everything you have right now can only bring you more, because your heart is open to more.

> *The expression of gratitude is a powerful force that generates even more of what we have already received. If you create any open space within yourself, love will fill it.*
> —Deepak Chopra

Exercise 5-4
What I'm Grateful For Right Now

Make a decision to expand your gratitude starting here and now. Make a list of things you're grateful for. Not only the obvious things like home, material

---

possessions and loved ones, but also gifts of nature, your physical and mental capabilities, and anything you may tend to take for granted. Then make it a habit to come back and read this list every day. And add to it as time goes on.

_____

_____

_____

_____

_____

_____

_____

_____

_____

_____

_____

_____

_____

_____

_____

_____

_____

_____

_____

_____

_____

CHAPTER SIX

Step Six
Act

I think there is something more important than believing. Action! The world is full of dreamers; there aren't enough who will move ahead and begin to take concrete steps to actualize their vision.
— W. Clement Stone

You can make decisions, you can build belief, you can create beautiful visualizations, and you can say affirmations all day long. But nothing will happen until you act, will it. (No, I didn't forget the question mark here. I don't need to ask you what you already know. I need to state the obvious as an all-important reminder of an all-important truth.)

Action is the physical manifestation of intent. Or to put it less elegantly, it's where the rubber meets the road.

Action is the real measure of intelligence.
— Napoleon Hill

And even though the discussion of taking action is near the end of this book, it's the first thing to do after deciding on your goal. You take immediate action, and you persist in taking action consistently every day. All six steps will dance with one another in different combinations to different music at different times along the way, and all the while, you are in action.

So far we've focused on what might be called "the art of deliberate creation:" how to dream in ways that build foundations in your mind and heart for taking immediate, effective, and sustained action. Now let's see what it takes to stand tall upon those foundations and secure a solid foothold for ascending to the realization of your dream.

> *I have been impressed with the urgency of doing. Knowing is not enough; we must apply. Being willing is not enough; we must do.*
> —Leonardo da Vinci

THE FIVE Ws AND THE H: A FORMULA FOR CREATING PLANS

Who, What, Where, When, Why and How. An ancient Greek formula for getting the whole story. It began as a way to analyze circumstances. It evolved across the centuries through many applications from Bible study and law to forensics and elementary education. In early 20th century America it became a journalistic principle requiring reporters to exert the utmost discipline and craftsmanship. They had to fit the answers to all five Ws and the H into the first sentence of a newspaper story. I won't ask you to do that, but as this formula works for many things, let's use it for creating your plan.

Exercise 6-1:
What's Your Plan?

Who are you, What do you want, Where do you want it, When do you want it, Why do you want it, and How do you propose to get it? Your answers should relate to the one goal you chose to focus on in Chapter One, Exercise 1-9. Now write your answers below.

Who Am I?

In Chapter One you defined these special things about yourself: Who you are in terms of your values, your special talents, your life's Definite Major Purpose, what you do best, and who you want to become. Now write it again here.

_____

_____

_____

_____

_____

What Do I Want?

Now describe the goal you chose in Chapter One in detail. An example of the level of detail would be that if you want a new home, specify the house and lot size, number of bedrooms and baths, number of stories, number of cars the garage will hold, the view, if there's a swimming pool, tennis court, etc. Or another example would be simply, "I want to be debt free and financially independent with an annual income of X dollars."

_____

_____

_____

_____

Where Do I Want It?

Depending on what your goal is, your answer could be anything from "In my life" to "In my bank account" to "In Tahiti."

_____

When Do I Want It?

Write down the date you specified in Chapter One.

_____

Why Do I Want It?

What does it achieve for you in terms of your daily life, your values and your life's purpose? How will you and others benefit? If your goal is money, what will you do with it? How will that make you feel?

_____

_____

_____

_____

How Do I Expect to Get It?

Summarize the actions you believe you should take; who you will tell; who you might ask to help or mentor you; what you know you must overcome; and *what you're willing to do* in order to make space for your dream to come true.

_____

_____

_____

_____

You've just created a plan that lets you see "the whole story" quite concisely. Now let's look at what it takes to execute your plan.

THE ART OF TAKING ACTION

Just as there's an art to productive dreaming, there's an art to taking action, and it's based on managing your attitude, forming productivity habits, planning, tracking and managing your progress, and persistently taking action.

The top five action-taking attitudes are:

- Courage
- Purposefulness
- Willingness to do whatever it takes
- Patience
- Persistence

The top five productivity habits are:

- Consistency
- Efficiency
- Effectiveness
- Managing/tracking/measuring
- Sense of urgency

Recognizing Fear

In a paper called *The Common Denominator of Success,* Albert E.N. Gray wrote, "The secret of success of every man who has ever been successful lies in the fact that he has formed the habit of doing things that failures don't like to do." Above all else, this includes stepping out of your comfort zone into the unknown, and doing things you may fear.

Fear is guaranteed the minute you decide to create something new and big in your life. You may fear your very ability to act in the first place. You may fear making mistakes, being embarrassed, looking foolish, losing face. And of course, you'll be afraid of failing. Your Inner Critic is hard at work here.

As if your own natural fears are not enough, there are the "outer critics" too. They're always there to "help." They'll say you can't do it, or you shouldn't do it, or the timing isn't right, or people don't succeed at those things. Whatever. They know not what they do. They are stepping on your dream.

> *Whatever course you decide upon, there is someone to tell you that you are wrong. There are always difficulties arising which tempt you to believe your critics are right. To map out a course of action and follow it to an end requires courage.*
> —Ralph Waldo Emerson

Fear is the Number One enemy of courage. Fear is the Number One enemy of action. Fear is immobilizing.

> *The greatest barrier to success is the fear of failure.*
>
> —Sven Goran Eriksson

Fear often comes disguised as some "necessary" activity like "getting ready" to take action.

It's one thing to have your ducks lined up. It's another to be in a protracted state of "getting ready" to take action. The victims of this trick feel compelled to organize their desks, organize their offices, organize their houses and organize their garages before acting upon what they're supposed to be acting upon ... if ever! They feel they can't act upon the real objective until everything else "aligns" perfectly. They're getting ready to get ready to get ready. Days and weeks go by. They think they're taking action, but they're really waiting for the perfect storm. In most cases this means they're afraid. Has fear ever tricked you this way?

Enter overwhelm.

Overwhelm can trip you up at this or any point in your journey, but it's most prominent when you decide to grow or stretch your life beyond its current limits.

Frequently the gap between where you are and where you want to be is so big that you assume your first steps must be big also. Overwhelm sets in and you freeze.

Know this: You don't have to take huge steps. You don't have to go all or nothing. You don't have to be crushed beneath a cascading pile of "too much to do" until you simply shut down and do nothing.

Overwhelm is only a feeling; a phantom; a mind game.

You only have to take the first small step, and the next small steps, one at a time. It's the small incremental steps that get you where you want to go. Do a little something every day instead of doing nothing because you allowed overwhelm to freeze you. This will release you from overwhelm's trap.

As mentioned elsewhere, I'm a big fan of massive action but even massive action is a series of small incremental steps taken in rapid succession.

You have everything within you to achieve your biggest, most audacious goals and you will achieve them one step at a time. In the words often attributed to Lao-tzu, *A journey of a thousand miles begins with a single step.* Take it!

Naysayers, procrastination, overwhelm—they're all a part of fear—and if you allow them to block you from taking action, obviously you can't succeed. So you've got to be willing to *unplug* from all that, fumble your way in if necessary, and then stumble along the way.

> *It is not the critic who counts: not the man who points out how the strong man stumbles or where the doer of deeds could have done better. The credit belongs to the man*

who is actually in the arena, whose face is marred by dust and sweat and blood, who strives valiantly, who errs and comes up short again and again, because there is no effort without error or shortcoming, but who knows the great enthusiasms, the great devotions, who spends himself for a worthy cause; who, at the best, knows, in the end, the triumph of high achievement, and who, at the worst, if he fails, at least he fails while daring greatly, so that his place shall never be with those cold and timid souls who knew neither victory nor defeat.

–Theodore Roosevelt

Here. Try this affirmation on for size:

I know what to do and I do it.

Getting Past the Fear

My friend and success coach Lisa Jimenez says fear is your "green light to go." The idea is that if you're not feeling some fear regularly, you're lingering too much in your comfort zone. Fear is the natural result of expanding your life. So when you feel fear, embrace it, and go!

Welcome the fear. Welcome the uncertainty. If you don't feel them, your goal isn't big enough. Fear and uncertainty go hand-in-hand with creating something great. Learn to view them as a natural part of expanding and growing, and then get past them by *taking action.*

As Susan Jeffers said in her book, *Feel the Fear and Do It Anyway*, "The only way to get rid of the fear of doing something is to go out and do it." It's that simple. Taking action changes everything.

> *Action conquers fear.*
> —Peter Nivio Zarlenga

I believe in taking immediate, massive action. Especially for big goals. But just any degree of action is all it takes to break the chains of fear and set you on your way. So don't hesitate!

> *To begin with fault is better than to hesitate perfectly.*
> —Author unknown

Right on, don't you think? Right on! Remember that quotation and say it back to your Inner Critic when it starts reciting all the reasons not to act! And say it whenever fear comes arrogantly marching in disguised as "getting ready."

Give yourself permission to be imperfect. Even if your move into action is sloppy or in the wrong direction, it's still action. It has more energy than inaction. And don't view any setbacks as failures. Take them as feedback. Take them in stride. You're just learning what works and what doesn't.

*Anything worth doing is worth doing poorly
until you learn to do it well.*
                                   –Steve Brown

When you're willing to step into the unknown and take some degree of action every day, it expands who you are. You're not sitting back and floating aimlessly through meaningless days that turn into weeks that turn into months. If you do something that scares you, it keeps you on your toes. It keeps you in the game. It keeps you searching. It keeps you young. So ...

Do something you're afraid of every day.
                                   –Eleanor Roosevelt

Don't worry about failing. Worry about the opportunities you'll miss if you don't even try.

Getting Off Your Duff Daily

Once you've broken the chains of fear and moved into action, you must continue taking action every day. Anyone can take a few steps toward a goal, but the one who takes consistent action daily is the one who wins the prize.

Suppose you're a sculptor whose life purpose is the creation of great works in stone that will last forever. Your current goal or *definite purpose* is to create a life-size sculpture of a local hero, and you want to donate it to your community as a complete surprise on opening day of this year's annual community fair. This decision is a promise to yourself. Fulfilling this promise means you'll have to chip away at that piece of stone for X days at X hours per day *consistently* until you've transformed it into a *result*. If you miss a day, you'll have to do twice as much the next day or you'll miss your deadline and you haven't kept your promise. But you prefer to keep your promises, don't you.

> *Often, we make commitments to ourselves— such as setting goals or making New Year's resolutions—that we fail to fulfill. As a result, we come to feel that we can't even fully trust ourselves. If we can't trust ourselves, we'll have a hard time trusting others. This personal incongruence is often the source of our suspicions of others. As my father often said, we judge ourselves by our intentions and others by their behavior. This is why ... one of the fastest ways to restore trust is to make and keep commitments—even very small commitments—to ourselves and to others.*
>
> —Stephen M. R. Covey

Being Consistent

Albert E. N. Gray deftly tied the idea of *definite purpose, decision, promise* and *consistency* together in one beautiful package containing the most exciting *result* possible when he wrote this: "Any resolution or decision you make is simply a promise to yourself which isn't worth a tinker's damn unless you have formed the habit of making it and keeping it. You won't form the habit of making it and keeping it unless right at the start you link it with a definite purpose that can be accomplished by keeping it.

"In other words, any resolution or decision you make today has to be made again tomorrow, and the next day, and the next day, and the next and so on. And it not only has to be made each day but it has to be kept each day for if you miss one day in the making or the keeping of it, you've got to go back and begin it all over again. But if you continue the process of making it in the morning and keeping it each day *you will finally wake up some morning a different man in a different world and you will wonder what has happened to you and the world you used to live in.*" (The italics are mine.)

And so, success is made of many small steps that make a big difference. One small step each day can make the difference for all of your tomorrows. Don't underestimate the value of small incremental gains and how they play out over time. And by the way, beware of the all-or-nothing mentality, where you're not satisfied with small steps so you wind up doing nothing at all.

Your progress may be arduous at first. You may even feel as if you're running up a down escalator.

Whenever you're creating space for something new in your life, there will be growing pains. But you're also learning what to do and what not to do; you know which steps you should repeat; and you're developing your strength and your skills.

Without consistency, there is no prize.

Gaining Momentum

When you take some kind of action consistently every day, you'll start seeing intermediate outcomes all along the pathway toward your goal. That's when this beautiful thing called "momentum" so magically comes into play. The up escalator becomes a downhill slide. Going down that slide becomes natural to you, and fun! Ease and joy ultimately become part of the process. Skills or aptitudes that you may have lacked in the beginning will now be second nature to you. Be patient.

> *Great acts are made up of small deeds.*
> –Lao Tzu

Once you hit your stride and momentum is on your side, things often start to happen without you. Some of it is serendipitous; things that were simply meant to be. Some may seem to be misfortunes, but may actually yield fortuitous outcomes across the trajectory of time.

Taking "Inspired" Action

Let's take a look at the difference between "action" and "inspired" action.

"Action" is, of course, the practical stuff that each day's To Do list is made of.

"Inspired" action is this little blip of light or this nudge that comes from out of "nowhere" for reasons you don't immediately understand. Like, something tells you to call Sarah. You haven't talked to her in two years.

The thing about inspired actions is that you need to act on them immediately. They come with an early expiration date; a small window of opportunity before their hidden purpose becomes obsolete. Don't ask me why. Nobody knows why. It's simply the perfect time to call Sarah. Stop what you're doing and call Sarah before the window closes.

And don't worry about why this inspiration hit you. If you don't know why, then the deeper purpose beyond "just getting in touch" is hidden at first. So don't analyze. Just follow your intuition. You never know where this will lead. You could wind up with some unexpected benefit. Maybe you're popping into Sarah's life just when she needed your unique knowledge about something. Or maybe she knows how to solve some problem that had been worrying you. All of that is serendipity.

Inspired actions and the experiences they spawn usually begin as a collection of seemingly disconnected threads that turn out to be a perfectly logical tapestry of beneficial outcomes—all of it beyond our control or understanding. The same is true of unexpected events that seemed disastrous when they occurred but were "meant to be" because they eventually resulted in favorable outcomes that no one could have possibly imagined in advance.

The "Maybe Yes Maybe No" story is a powerful example of how useless it is to pre-judge or over-analyze the meaning of things we can't hope to understand.

In "Maybe Yes Maybe No," a farmer's only horse ran away. That evening the neighbors came over to sympathize. "This is such bad luck! Your farm will suffer if you cannot plow," they said. "Surely this is a terrible thing to have happened to you."

"Maybe yes, maybe no," the farmer said.

The next day, the horse returned and brought with it six wild horses. The neighbors came to congratulate the farmer and marvel at his fortune. "You're richer than you were before," they said. "Surely this has turned out to be a good thing for you after all."

"Maybe yes, maybe no," the farmer said.

The next day, his son tried to saddle and ride one of the wild horses. He was thrown and broke his leg, so he couldn't work on the farm. Again the neighbors came over to offer their sympathy. "There's more work than you can possibly handle, poor farmer! What will you do? You'll be driven into poverty and misfortune. This is terrible!"

"Maybe yes, maybe no," the farmer said.

The next day, some conscription officers came to the village to take young men for the Army, but they didn't take the farmer's son because of his broken leg. When the neighbors came again they said, "How fortunate! Things have worked out for you after all! Most young men may never return alive from the war. Surely this is the best of fortunes for you."

"Maybe yes, maybe no," the farmer said.

And so, don't judge. The story is not all told. We need to stay loose in our judgment of everything because we never know which undesirable circumstances may yield desirable results.

Maybe you can remember times in your life when something awful had turned into a blessing and you said in utter astonishment, "Now I know why it all happened the way it did! They were meant to be, or this wonderful (you fill in the blank) would never have been possible!" I bet that's happened to you before, and I bet it will happen again.

Exercise 6-2
Finding the Hidden Gifts

Take a moment and think about a past or current situation so disastrous that you couldn't see anything positive about it. You couldn't even see the light at the end of a tunnel. It turned your world upside down. Looking back, see if you can sift out some gift or positive outcome that eventually occurred as a result. Make a habit of doing this. There are most always hidden gifts that we can't see when we're in the thick of it. What was the situation and what was the hidden gift?

_____

_____

_____

_____

_____

_____

Please visit
http://www.absolutelyanythingyouwant.com to download printable PDF copies of this exercise.

Where to Begin Taking Action

This question applies to two phases of action-taking. First there's the action you take immediately after deciding on your goal. Then there's the first step you choose from the To Do list that keeps you taking action consistently every day.

For your "immediate action" step, simply start where you are, do what you know, give it everything you've got, and the rest will come as you proceed. You don't need all the answers up front in order to begin.

Whatever you can do or dream you can, begin it. Boldness has genius, power, and magic in it.

—Johann Wolfgang von Goethe

No matter how big and lofty my dream, I've never had a situation where I couldn't come up with at least one action step to get me started, even if it was just talking with someone who had been there done that. And then acting upon their advice. I'm sure this is also true for you. I believe that if the decision you made about your goal was a quality decision, you won't have any trouble knowing what to do first, and doing it immediately.

For your daily list of actions, start with either the most challenging or the most valuable one. Maybe they're one-and-the-same. Let's define them this way:

- "most valuable" is the one with the highest payoff;
- "most challenging" is the biggest, hardest, most fearsome of them all.

Choose the one that makes you go *gulp*. The Big One that most people put off. "I must get to that. I must get to that." Putting off the Big One only builds anxiety about when you're going to face up to it. Don't put yourself through that. Dive in. Tackle it. Obviously, this gets you into the zone. It sets the tone for further action. You'll feel good and confident about yourself, and you'll make the most meaningful progress.

THE REGULAR HABITS THAT MATTER

Motivate Yourself

You can't depend on anyone else to motivate you. Your motivation must spring from deep inside. It's a product of how you feel about what you're doing. It draws its strength from your constant awareness of your Definite Major Purpose, your passion for your goal, your determination to achieve it, and your vow to keep your promises. If you make it a habit to consistently see yourself and your every move as being purpose-driven instead of task-driven, you'll stay motivated and you'll enjoy your every task.

> *Motivation is what gets you started. Habit is what keeps you going.*
> —Jim Rohn

Just Say No

When creating something new, you have to make room for it, and I don't mean clearing out your garage! Clear out your mental, emotional, and activity space of things that no longer serve you. Some things may be "good" but you've outgrown them without realizing it. Get rid of the "good" so you can make room for the "best."

Exercise 6-3
From Now On I Say No To:

What no longer fits, excites or resonates with you? List as many as you can think of here:

_____

_____

_____

_____

_____

_____

_____

_____

Establish a Morning Practice

Devote the first waking moments of each new day to personal enrichment: a regular morning practice of studying inspirational material, meditating or praying, affirming, and journaling.

- Reconnect with your Definite Major Purpose
- Realign with and expand your vision
- Read and repeat your affirmations

Use Your Calendar
To Keep Up with Yourself

Use your calendar for more than the usual entries. Here's an example.

Let's say you've scheduled yourself to attend an educational or training event. Are you making sure you'll get a good return on the investment of time and money spent? That is, will your mind be cleared and ready to receive new information on arrival? Or do you usually arrive on one wheel while shifting gears at the last minute from some other activity? And then after the event is behind you, do you do anything with what you've learned?

For me, calendaring is the answer. When I book an event on my calendar, I also block out some extra time around it. First I schedule at least 30 minutes before the event to quietly sit down and prepare myself mentally for it. I shut out all distractions and focus on my intention for being there. What do I want to get out of this event?

At the same time I also schedule at least a couple of hours as soon after the event as possible to review what I learned and what I must do next to implement it. I will have taken very good notes at the event and put a triple star next to every action item. So when I do sit down for my pre-scheduled review, I see the action items readily and get them into my calendar too.

Stuff really gets done this way. I can no longer count on "maybe I'll have time tomorrow." If it gets in my calendar, it's as good as done. If it doesn't, it probably won't.

Make Every Move And Every Moment Count

Think of every move you can make to increase your efficiency and productivity. This includes:

- leveraging the efforts of others by outsourcing certain activities;
- performing prime activities in prime time.

Do the most important things when you're freshest. Of these tasks, tackle the hardest one first. Scratching these items off your To Do list will not only advance your daily progress; it will also boost both your momentum and your morale.

> *The key is not to prioritize what's on your schedule, but to schedule your priorities.*
> –Stephen R. Covey

Track Your Progress

While this is obviously not a book on business or time management, and even if your dream has nothing to do with building a business, I'm suggesting that you approach your entire goal-seeking process as if it were a business. So your productivity habits would include the continuous management of your activities and the measuring of your progress in a way that reveals what you should or should not be doing to achieve your result.

Keep a daily journal, or a spread sheet, or whatever it takes to continuously keep track of what's going on in the service of your purpose. You've committed to a specific goal and a specific deadline for achieving it. Document the action steps you've taken. They've gotten you this far and yielded such-and-such results. You still need to go this much farther. So you need to do more of this, less of that, or ten times as much of something else. Always have a clear picture of where you stand and what you'll need to do in order to keep your commitment.

Maintain a Constant Sense of Urgency

Oh, you have so precious little time to fulfill your purpose, to make your difference in this world, to get absolutely everything you want!

> *Make haste! The tide of Fortune soon ebbs.*
> —Silius Italicus

The Roman orator and Latin poet of the first century CE wrote that in his 12,000-line poem, Punica, some time between the year 83 and 103. Nothing about the goal-seeker's need for a constant sense of urgency has changed since then.

If you really really want what you say you want, you must regard everything as urgent, and urgency as everything. From breaking through the fear barriers and taking immediate action the minute you know your goal, to what you do each day toward achieving it, urgency is everything.

> *I've continued to recognize the power individuals have to change virtually anything and everything in their lives in an instant. I've learned that the resources we need to turn our dreams into reality are within us, merely waiting for the day when we decide to wake up and claim our birthright.*
>
> –Anthony Robbins

How profound. That isn't fluff. Tony Robbins has coached millions and has seen countless demonstrations of this fact: The power is there within you. The resources are within you! So there's nothing to wait for! And it's urgent! Roll up your sleeves, do whatever it takes, and persist.

Whatever It Takes, Do It

You must be sure at the starting line that you're prepared to go the distance, and that you're willing to do whatever it takes in order to keep your promise.

In the early days of building my business, my Whatever-it-Takes consisted of driving very long distances to put on presentations because I couldn't afford to fly; and sleeping in my car because I couldn't afford hotels. And my Sacrifice was having to leave my little kids behind.

When an interviewer once asked, "How did it make you feel about yourself ... sleeping in your car and getting dressed in gas station restrooms back in the day," I knew what she was getting at. No, I didn't feel disenfranchised. No, I didn't feel victimized. I didn't give it a thought. It was just what had to be done. I was so focused on the finish line that my comfort at any given moment was not an issue.

I was willing to travel any distance to do a presentation. From Utah to California, Arizona, Nevada, New Mexico and Kentucky I rolled in my little Subaru wagon. Whatever it took, I'd be there. I would arrive bursting with enthusiasm and conviction saying, "Join me. We're going to become millionaires!" And sometimes I would find an audience of two instead of the packed house that was promised. Once I drove nearly three hours, only to find an audience of none.

The biggest sacrifice, though, was the loss of time with my kids. One evening after kissing them goodnight, leaving them with a babysitter and pulling out of the garage to go make a presentation, I saw little three-year-old Todd running out of the house in his bare feet and pajamas.

"Mommy don't go! Mommy don't go!" he cried.

I pulled the car over and got out and held him close long enough to compose myself so I could speak. "Hey Todd, go inside and be a big boy and I promise, I *promise* you that someday I'll take you everywhere I go!" But at that moment I had no idea how I would ever fulfill that promise.

He was crying so hard, he didn't notice that I was crying too.

The last thing I wanted was to leave those kids for a meeting where who knew if anyone would come, who knew how many might be there, who knew if anyone would join me. My Whatever-it-Takes was profoundly challenged, but I had to go on and I would have to keep on going on. That night was one of those "razor's edge" actions for me.

The Razor's Edge Actions

This is that extra action you take when you feel you can't go another inch. It's the family you leave at home when you need to go out on business. It's that extra phone call you make when you've already pushed beyond your limit. It's the very last thing on today's To Do list—that thing you'd rather do tomorrow, or not do at all. It's that discipline ... that refusal to give up ... that price you pay ... the extra few percent that you almost didn't give for the gold vein that yes, you finally do uncover!

I paid the price and was rewarded a thousand-fold when the day arrived that I could keep the promise I had made to little pajama-clad Todd that night on the sidewalk in front of our home. Since those days I've been able to take all four of my kids all over the place! Western and Eastern Europe, Egypt, China, Asia, Southeast Asia, Fiji, Australia, New Zealand, Mexico, Alaska and more.

Still, there is an even greater reward than the money and personal freedom that came from paying the price. If you should ask me what is the most important thing I've gained from all the Whatever-it-Takes and all the Razor's Edge actions, it's who I've become in the process. This is huge compared to the price. This is the reward that keeps returning on your investment. This is the reward that lasts.

When you call on yourself to perform in a big way despite the price, and when you go the distance no matter the pain, this builds the self-confidence that is central to who you're becoming. The inner knowledge that you've kept your promises and that you can count on yourself to come through will stay with you forever. *Who you become* is a profound and priceless resource that you can draw upon any time to support your continuing success.

Observe the Law
of the Harvest

The Law of the Harvest states, "There is a sowing season and a reaping season, and it is not in the same
season." Remember this all along the way. Whenever
you feel impatient, whenever you feel your progress is
too slow, whenever you feel you've done all you can
and the reaping will never come, remember this: All
you can do is keep planting. You can't know which
seeds will bear fruit; how many seeds you'll have to
plant; when the reaping will come; or where it will
come from.

Know this: The harvest will be commensurate with
the planting. And you just have to keep planting—
without counting today's results and revenues—until
the reaping season arrives.

I kept on planting seeds long after I'd made my
first million. That was just an intermediate goal along
the way. One seed that I planted in New York City pro-
duced a harvest beyond anything I could have ever
imagined. In fact, I expected no harvest at all.

I was asked to present my business opportunity to
a fairly good-sized audience. I flew in hours before
the meeting, leaving ample time to take a cab, but the
driver got lost en route. I arrived 30 minutes late to
find an irritated crowd of people vigorously fanning
themselves in a hot, stuffy meeting room.

Convinced that this audience couldn't be salvaged, I kept the presentation short, and stuck around for questions.

A Russian gentleman came up and said in a thick accent, "I vant to take dis to Russia."

I had reached a point in my career where I no longer counted on what people said. I now waited for their actions. So I patted him on the shoulder and said "Great! You do that! Let me know if I can help you!"

Within a few months I started noticing these names on my monthly team member summary: Svetlana, Igor, Pisarevsky, Valentin—there were pages of them. And every month there were more and more pages. Soon I was making over $30,000 a month more than before that New York presentation!

By now I knew my business had spread all over Eurasia. I had team members in Ukraine, Kazakhstan, Republic of Georgia, Latvia, Uzbekistan and Siberia. Finally I decided to order the full printout of team members so I could see the whole picture.

The report arrived in a big box. It was printed on that old green and white accordion-folded computer paper with 50 names between perforations. I took it out of the box, put it on my desk, and it stood nine or ten inches tall. One half *million* Russian distributors were on my marketing team! I had planted a seed in New York, and it multiplied as a piece of Eurasia.

How could I have possibly imagined such an outcome during those days of planting seeds that never sprouted. All those meetings with attendance of few to none—compared to this event—were they not like the story of the Chinese bamboo?

It's been said that there's a bamboo tree in China that shows no evidence of growth for the first five years despite constant care and feeding. But in the fifth year, watch out! Suddenly it starts growing as much as three feet per day, soon reaching a height of 90 feet or more. Yet it would never have grown an inch if it had been neglected during those first five years.

There is a sowing season and a reaping season and they are not the same season. For those who keep on planting and nurturing and doing whatever it takes consistently, the reaping season comes. It's a natural law of the universe. And the harvest belongs to the persistent.

> *As long as we are persistent in our pursuit of our deepest destiny, we will continue to grow. We cannot choose the day or time when we will fully bloom. It happens in its own time.*
>
> —Denis Waitley

Persist

When you perform an action, you learn whether or not it works. If it didn't work, don't think of it as a failure.

Think of it as feedback. And yes I've said that before. Don't even think in terms of success or failure. Think in terms of persistently moving forward with whatever *does* work. Remember that Thomas Edison "got feedback" 10,000 times before he perfected the incandescent light bulb. He simply refused to give up.

> *Nothing in the world can take the place of Persistence. Talent will not; nothing is more common than unsuccessful people with talent. Genius will not; unrewarded genius is almost a proverb. Education will not; the world is full of educated derelicts. Persistence and determination alone are omnipotent. The slogan 'Press On' has solved and always will solve the problems of the human race.*
>
> –President Calvin Coolidge

By Pressing On, Thomas Edison finally brought the world out of darkness.

By Pressing On, tens of thousands of American citizens developed the means to break the bond of Earth's gravity, send the first humans to our moon, and return them safely.

By Pressing On, the "you" in Albert E.N. Gray's example of consistency and persistence could "wake up some morning a different man in a different world, wondering whatever happened to you and the world you used to live in."

By Pressing On, you are, as TV game show host Peter Marshall put it, the oak "growing strong in contrary winds." And he reminded us that "diamonds are made under pressure."

> *I will persist until I succeed. Always will I take another step. If that is of no avail I will take another, and yet another. In truth, one step at a time is not too difficult. ... I know that small attempts, repeated, will complete any undertaking.*
>
> –Og Mandino

When my 19-year-old daughter Ashley and I hiked Taylor Creek in Kolob Canyon at the north end of Zion National Park, I thought we'd be completing a five-mile round trip. Ashley, however, thought it was five miles each way. So she assumed that we probably wouldn't finish but that we'd go as far as we wanted to, and then we'd turn around.

After we'd been hiking for quite some time, Ashley said, "So Mom, we've come quite a long way; maybe we should go back now."

"Oh Ashley I'd really like to finish," I replied.

"Mom, we're not gonna finish a ten-mile hike this morning!"

I let her know that it was a five-mile round trip, not five miles each way, and suggested that we keep going for another 10 or 15 minutes. If we weren't at the top by that time, or feeling we were close, we could reassess.

Just as we reached that 15-minute mark, we passed a family coming down. We asked them how close we were to the top, and if it was worth it. They said "Oh you're so close. You've come this far, you've got to finish because it really is worth it! It's beautiful up there!"

With renewed determination and vigor we decided to press on to the top.

And so it is with life. Whenever you do something for the first time, you have no idea how long it will take. You don't know what signs to look for along the way, so you don't know how close you are to the finish. Many people stop short of success because they're tired of the climb and they feel their destination is simply out of reach, when truly, success may be just around the corner.

We made it to the top, and it was fantastic. Sheer cliffs of red rock seeping waters of iridescent gold, green and amber—it's spectacular and unforgettable. And as we went back down we encouraged everyone we passed to keep going. "Keep going! It's beautiful! It's worth it!"

Persist.

> *Before success comes to any man's life, he*
> *is sure to meet with much temporary defeat*
> *and perhaps some failure. When defeat*

overtakes a man, the easiest and most logical thing to do is quit. That is what the majority of most men do.

–Napoleon Hill

When the going gets the toughest, when you feel challenged to the max, remember that progress doesn't come from comfort. It springs from your ability to endure the process of leaving your comfort zone to grow, and expand, and reach for your highest good.

My son Shaun came to see this after walking a destructive path during his high school years. He had found a comfort zone in the company of friends who were not going where he wanted to go in life. Yet as he matured and began to realize he had chosen the wrong direction, he started making some constructive decisions for himself.

Instinctively he put one foot in front of the other with remarkable steadiness as he chose the first and second and third right action to take. On and on he progressed, doing enough right stuff until one day, just as E. N. Gray had written about consistency, Shaun had become one of those people to "finally wake up some morning a different man in a different world," wondering what had happened to him and the world he used to live in. I thought of that when I visited him in his beautiful corner office in that Long Beach high-rise not long ago. There he was with an important position, fulfilling work and a great salary to go with it.

By age 28 Shaun had turned from the dark pathways to nowhere and deliberately created a completely new world for himself. A world of achievement and abundance with plenty of room for more, by taking action and doing enough right stuff. Consistently and persistently.

And so, no matter what, take action, be consistent, and persist.

I've always believed that I may not be the fastest, the smartest or the best, but I'll win because I won't quit.

MASTERMINDING AS AN ACTION-TAKING TOOLSET

When you need to take action on anything at any point of any journey, nothing beats being in a mastermind group. The very process is like having a set of certain tools for different tasks. You can pry yourself out of isolation ... wrench yourself from stuck to unstuck ... drill down into a topic ... hammer out a plan ... hack away a bad idea ... cut through to a great inspiration and so on, just by talking and listening and brainstorming in a purposeful group setting.

Napoleon Hill introduced me to the principles of masterminding way back when I first read *Think and Grow Rich* years ago. I learned that masterminding gives us free access to a collective pool of information, experience and creative thinking by people who share similar goals. We can view our challenges and opportunities through the eyes of caring, likeminded people. They become our circle of safety, enabling us to openly share our issues, seek advice, and gain fresh perspectives. And the participants often become a rich resource of contacts within their own circles, potentially opening doors and new relationships all around.

> *No two minds ever come together without, thereby, creating a third, invisible, intangible force which may be likened to a third mind.*
> –Napoleon Hill

Strong stuff, that "third mind" concept, to say the least. Not only does masterminding make you take action. Its benefits are profound and virtually open-ended.

I first began participating in a formalized mastermind group about 15 years ago. Today I can credit masterminding with some of the best things that have happened to me in business and in life.

And how about having more than one mastermind group for more than one purpose! Now we're talking. Currently I have three.

One of my masterminds is now seven years old. We first met at a high-level business seminar where the attendees were assigned to mastermind groups of six for one year. Our group kept it going for several years thereafter. To this day, three of us meet at least once monthly, and to this day every call is exciting. We're all in different businesses and in different phases of life, yet we mutually understand our business and personal lives because we've been sharing it all for so long. It's awesome how we've seen each other through so many challenges and triumphs. We've also been able to open doors for each other with introductions to our contacts among thought leaders in different fields. All of this has translated into extraordinary mutual support.

My second mastermind consists of four women in network marketing. One is a speaker/coach, and three are marketers, all with different parent companies. We just celebrated one member's first six-figure month— an achievement she realized from scratch in a mere three years. Another member has been in network marketing since she was 19, and has just had her first child. I'm able to share my 24 years of experience in network marketing and in balancing business with family life. In turn I'm learning a lot from the other members. And since we've all achieved a similar level of success and know the nuts and bolts of creating a successful business, we're able to focus on high-level issues requiring specific and targeted advice.

My third mastermind consists of three movers and shakers who are participating in a year-long training program about branding. Since we're all studying the same material and want to implement it, we took the initiative of forming a mastermind to deepen our learning. We meet once a week to hold one another accountable for moving through the modules; to discuss how the program is working in our businesses; and to help one another advance to the next stage of our respective endeavors.

And so, some of the best ideas behind the success I enjoy today have come from masterminding. And I've met many amazing people as a result of mastermind referrals that have opened door after door after door. I can only look forward with great delight to a whole lot more.

> *You are the same today as you will be in five years except for two things: the people you meet and the books you read.*
> –Charlie "Tremendous" Jones

Exercise 6-4:
The Action Wheel

Whenever I undertake a new major project, I fill in the blanks in an action wheel. This one's for you. Write your goal in the center, then fill each spoke of the wheel with action steps for achieving it. Make sure you take one or two actions within the next 24 hours.

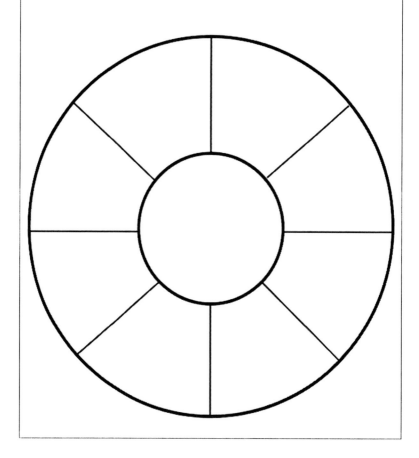

CHAPTER SEVEN

Be Grateful

Be thankful for what you have and you will end up having more. But if you concentrate on what you don't have, you'll never, ever have enough.

—Oprah Winfrey

Gratefulness is the quintessential quality that must be omnipresent in you. I said it up front and promised to say it again: You can't attract what you don't have yet if you're not grateful for what you have now.

A consistently present attitude of gratitude is the key to a happy life. We have dreams and goals and desires that we know will make us happier. "I'll be happy if" I can leave this job. "I'll be happy when" the kids are raised. "I'll be happy when" I pay off the house. And so on. And happiness becomes this elusive thing in the future. But life is not a practice run. This is it. Right here. Right now.

So why should we "if" and "when" our happiness away to some unknown moment in the distance? Why not feel happiness today? Why not let happiness travel with us on the pathways toward the goals we seek? I believe that's possible if we live life with a grateful heart.

> *Happiness cannot be traveled to, owned, earned, worn or consumed. Happiness is the spiritual experience of living every minute with love, grace, and gratitude.*
> —Denis Waitley

How to See Your World

As you grow your deepest desires within you, view your world through child-like eyes. See everything as new and fresh. See the people and the things you tend to take for granted through eyes of gratitude, and relate to them with a grateful heart.

I love what Brother David Steindl-Rast said in his book *Gratefulness, the Heart of Prayer.* He links gratitude with surprise, and surprise with waking up. Waking up from what? From the death we die by taking things for granted.

He uses a rainbow as an example. He says a rainbow always comes as a surprise, and it has a way of waking us up from taking things for granted.

He says "Bored and boring adults become excited children" when they see a rainbow. "We might not understand what it was that startled us when we saw that rainbow. What was it? Gratuitousness burst in on us, the gratuitousness of all there is."

He encourages us to look at life with that same degree of surprise so we can see and experience the same old things that we experience day in and day out, but see them with a fresh perspective that enlivens us.

"What counts on our paths to fulfillment is that we remember the great truth that moments of surprise want to teach us," he writes. "Everything is gratuitous, everything is a gift. The degree to which we awake to this truth is the measure of our gratefulness, and gratefulness is the measure of our aliveness."

The Vibrational Frequencies of Thought

I believe, as many do, that our thoughts carry certain vibrations. There are low-frequency vibrations like shame, guilt, fear, anger, hatred etc.; and there are high-frequency vibrations like gratitude, love, bliss, optimism, resilience and perseverance in the face of disappointment. I also believe, as many do, that whatever those vibrations are, they attract more of the same back to us.

Gratefulness has such a high vibrational frequency that it can change most any state of mind and it can change whatever you're drawing to you in an instant. If you're feeling anxious, over-whelmed, disappointed, discouraged, irritated, mad, sad, whatever—you may not be able to suddenly switch to calm or peace or forgiveness. But you can always choose gratitude. And that shifts everything. You can recover in an instant by being grateful for what you have right now.

> *Gratitude unlocks the fullness of life. It turns what we have into enough, and more. It turns denial into acceptance, chaos into order, confusion into clarity. It can turn a meal into a feast, a house into a home, a stranger into a friend. Gratitude makes sense of our past, brings peace for today, and creates a vision for tomorrow.*
>
> —Melody Beattie

Choosing to feel grateful is so easy. And it simply changes everything.

> *You cannot be grateful and bitter.*
> *You cannot be grateful and unhappy.*
> *You cannot be grateful and without hope.*
> *You cannot be grateful and unloving.*
> *So just be grateful.*
>
> —Author unknown

Whatever you appreciate, you'll get more of. And you have much to be grateful for.

> *If you woke up this morning with more health than illness, you are more blessed*

than the million who will not survive the week. If you have food in your refrigerator, clothes on your back, a roof over your head and a place to sleep, you are richer than 75 percent of the world. If you have money in the bank or in your wallet, you are among the world's wealthy. If you hold up your head with a smile on your face and are truly thankful, you are blessed because the majority can, but most do not.

–Author unknown

The Ultimate Thank You

Every morning as you awaken, every night as you surrender to the stillness, and all throughout your days, let gratefulness wash over you and flood your mind, heart and soul with its warm and soothing essence. And always, express it liberally.

If the only prayer you ever say in your whole life is Thank you, that would suffice.

–Meister Eckhart

Epilogue

Finally, know this.

> *There are no secrets to success. It is the result of preparation, hard work, and learning from failure.*
>
> —Colin Powell

That's right. There are no secrets! The steps you've gone through in this book—that's it. That's all there is!

Don't wait around for any secrets. There are none. You began with a clear and unwavering statement of your purpose in life, and the decision to get what you want. You've built belief and vision. You've connected with your heart. Now, take action. Persist in taking action.

To take action, you must be fearless, you must be purpose-driven, you must be willing to sacrifice, and you must do whatever it takes. Urgently.

And you will not be denied. You will step into your place, you will live a life of purpose, you *will* get what you want, and you'll make a difference in this world.

About the Author

1939337From a lifetime of teaching, performing and mentoring, Margie Aliprandi brings heart and a unique perspective to her work as an author, trainer, and international speaker in the field of wealth coaching and personal development. To date she has played a significant role in the making of more than 1,000 millionaires.

Margie was crowned Miss Teenage Utah at the age of 14, and later became a Mrs. Utah. She has performed as a singer and actress on stage, and as a spokesperson in national radio and television commercials. In 1989 she left a music teaching career to establish what is today one of the world's largest direct sales organizations, spanning 29 countries with a team of over 250,000 for Utah-based Neways International. She achieved a five-figure monthly income within her first year, millionaire status within three years, and has been ranked number 61 among the top 500 earners in network marketing worldwide. Also listed among the top one percent of network marketing producers worldwide, she has earned every possible award from her company including the world's first rank of Crown Diamond.

Margie is the author of *Take Charge, Heal Yourself* and several training audios including *Millionaire Mindset, Energy of Success,* and *Six Steps to the Top of Your Pay Plan.* Her story has been featured in the movies *Pass It On Today* and *Go For No*; and in numerous publications including Libby Gill's *Capture the Mindshare and the Market Share Will Follow,* Richard Brookes' *Four Year Career,* John Milton Fogg's *Greatest Networkers in the World,* and *How to Become Filthy, Stinking Rich through Network Marketing* by Valerie Bates, Derek and Shelby Hall, and Mark Yarnell.

Margie spends her personal time at her home in Utah, or in Colorado, where her fiancé lives, or at her second home in California, where her children live. She loves yoga, walking, biking, hiking, boating, waterskiing, diving, gourmet cooking and throwing fabulous parties. Her four grown children are Shaun, Nicole, Todd and Ashley.

Margie travels internationally as a sought-after speaker on personal development, business and success principles, and optimal health. To engage her services as a speaker, you can reach her at 1-800-985-5711 or visit:

http://www.margiealiprandi.com

CPSIA information can be obtained at www.ICGtesting.com
Printed in the USA
BVOW070136110413

317818BV00001BB/55/P

9 781939 337429